W9-CKL-277

THE PICTORIAL
ENCYCLOPEDIA OF
CATS

THE PICTORIAL ENCYCLOPEDIA OF
CATS

BRITT STRADER

with the Photography of
ROBERT PEARCY

THUNDER BAY
P·R·E·S·S

This 1994 Edition published by
Thunder Bay Press
5880 Oberlin Drive, Suite 400
San Diego, California 92121

Produced by
Brompton Books Corporation
15 Sherwood Place,
Greenwich, Connecticut 06830

Copyright © 1989 Brompton Books Corporation

All rights reserved. No part of this publication may be
reproduced, stored in a retrieval system or transmitted in
any form by any means, electronic, mechanical,
photocopying or otherwise, without first obtaining written
permission of the copyright owner.

ISBN 934429-72-3

Printed in Hong Kong

Designed by Ruth DeJauregui
Edited by Joan Hayes
Captioned by Marie Cahill

All artwork courtesy of Dover, except for pages 9 and
10 which are courtesy of the American Graphic
Systems Archives.

Page 1: Though not a show cat, its grey
markings and vivid blue eyes make this household pet a beauty. *Page 2–3:* A Maine Coon,
the oldest longhaired breed in the United
States. *Page 4–5:* A Havana Brown.

CONTENTS

INTRODUCTION

Above: **A family of cats.** *Below:* **A typical Siamese, with large ears and long tail.** *Right:* **A kitten gingerly makes its way over a fence.**

Most authorities agree that today's domestic cat is descended from the African wild cat (*Felis silvestris libyca*). Bones of this cat have been found in the caves lived in by ancient man. It is unknown whether the cat was hunted and killed for food or whether its kittens were raised and tamed and used for pest control.

By 2500 BC in Egypt, when agriculture was well established there, silos full of grain attracted rats and mice, and tabbies, in turn, with very similar markings to those of the African wild cat, were tempted out of the woods by the rodents. Paintings and inscriptions from about this time show cats as domesticated animals. Because the cat meows, the Egyptians named it 'Mau.'

Soon after becoming useful members of Egyptian society, cats were accorded a place in religious ceremonies. The first official consecration of the cat in Egypt occurred when the Egyptian goddess Pasht, the symbol of fecundity and beauty, was depicted with the head of a cat. The word 'puss' may derive from her name. This beautiful and bewitching cat goddess next became the sun, moon, motherhood, and love goddess as well. She was born to rule, for her mother was Isis (goddess of the sun, moon, and earth) and her father was Ra (god of the sun and the underworld). Worship of Pasht and her representative, the cat, reached its peak around 950 BC, when more than 700,000 pilgrims traveled by boat each spring to Bubastis for her festival, which resembled Mardi Gras in New Orleans or Carnival in Rio.

There were two sorts of Egyptian cats: those with short ears and blunt noses and those with long ears and sharp noses. Most had short,

ginger-colored fur with black markings. They were pampered and protected by peasants and pharaohs alike. When a cat died, it was given an elaborate funeral, a wake was held, and its owners shaved their eyebrows to show their sorrow. It was illegal to harm a cat in Egypt, and the crime was punishable by death, even if it was an accident. According to Herodotus, one Roman soldier was torn to pieces by a maddened mob in Thebes after he accidentally killed a cat. Egyptians believed the goddess Pasht could transform herself into a cat; hence they were kind to all cats, thinking any one might be Pasht.

The custom of keeping cats gradually spread throughout the Middle East, and they either arrived in India and China sometime later than in Egypt or were separately tamed in those countries.

By about 100 BC, the cat cult in Egypt was in decline. Phoenician traders, who for years had been trying to smuggle cats to other parts of the world, where rats were an increasing problem, were finally able to export them in quantity.

Cats became popular in Europe in the first century AD. Pliny the Elder described their physical characteristics in his *Natural History,* and the Romans, in honor of the cat's independent nature, made the cat the symbol of liberty.

As the barbaric invasions brought rats and plague with them to the European continent in the fifth century AD, cats rose in value. Several countries had laws governing the sale of cats and for their protection.

This appreciation of the cat lasted for hundreds of years. At Moissac in France, a cat and her kittens are carved on a Romanesque capital. In a legend about St Francis of Assisi, a cat saves the animal-loving saint from a plague of mice by miraculously springing from his sleeve. Petrarch, the Italian poet, scholar, and patron of learning, loved his pet cat and, when Petrarch died, the cat was put to death and embalmed. Its mummy lies in a niche decorated with a marble cat and bearing a Latin inscription, said to have been written

At one time cats were erroneously associated with witchcraft (as seen in the drawing *at right*). The tiny fellow on the *facing page* will escape such a fate. *Below:* An American Shorthair.

by the poet himself, which declares the cat to have been 'second only to Laura,' his human love.

But by about the middle of the thirteenth century, the Church began to frown on the adoration of the cat, considering it too closely connected to paganism, and the cat became an outcast.

This change in attitude toward the cat was probably brought about by a return to the worship of Freya, the Scandinavian goddess of fertility, in whose rites the cat played a role. A total persecution of the cat was authorized by the Church and most of the people joined in. There was one big bonfire of heretics, witches, assassins and cats.

During Mary Tudor's reign, the cat was burned as a sign of the heresy of Protestantism, and during Elizabeth the First's reign as the symbol of the Catholic heresy. People believed witches could transform themselves into cats, which was another reason for the inhumane massacre. The Festival of St John, June 24, was particularly infamous, for on that day cats captured by the people were burned, flayed, crucified and thrown from the tops of towers.

By 1400 the cat was almost extinct in Europe. Paradoxically, the Black Death saved the cat, because, for lack of cats, two-thirds of the European population died of the plague. A few clear-thinking and brave individuals kept their cats, at total risk to themselves, and their homes and barns remained relatively rat free. Eventually, the authorities saw the light and stopped the terrible persecution of the cat.

From the end of the Renaissance on, the cat again became a valued member of society. Cardinal Wolsey, in England, took his cat with him to the cathedral and to conferences. Montaigne, Richelieu, and Mazarin, in France, enjoyed the company of cats. Richelieu bequeathed a large sum of money to his many cats so they would continue to be well cared for after his death.

During the eighteenth century Paradis de Moncrif wrote the first cat book, *Histoire des Chats*.

Above and below: **Folktales tell of the magical powers of cats.** *Right:* **A longhaired tabby in a typical cat pastime — sunning in the garden.**

The Victorian Age saw the cat re-established not only as a useful animal and pleasant pet, but also as a thing of beauty. It was fashionable to own a beautiful cat.

Harrison Weir, first president of the English National Cat Club, organized the first cat show at the Crystal Palace in London in 1871. An American version was held at Madison Square Garden in 1895. These two highly successful feline exhibitions have been followed by countless others.

In his 1889 book, *Our Cats and All About Them*, Harrison Weir wrote: 'Even the few instances of the shows generating a love for cats that have come before my own notice are a sufficient pleasure to me not to regret having thought out and planned the first Cat Show at the Crystal Palace.'

Seeing a variety of cats gathered together at the cat shows made people more aware of the different colors and patterns, and, as more was learned about genetics, cat fanciers became interested in creating new breeds and colors, and perfecting those already in existence. Since 1918 knowledge of genetics has continued to increase, and it is now possible to predict the kinds of kittens that will be produced in a given litter as to confirmation, color and length of fur.

Today the cat is a beloved pet in more and more homes, and is neither worshiped nor persecuted, but admired for its beauty and individual personality. And some cats, like some people, become rich and famous, such as *Morris*.

Cats are given to all kinds of moods — from philosophical to playful, as illustrated by this beautiful bicolor *(below)* **and tiny tabby** *(facing page)*.

THE PICTORIAL

ENCYCLOPEDIA

ABYSSINIAN

Owing to its ancestry and regal appearance, Abyssinian cat fanciers say: 'It is not a question of a simple cat, but of his majesty the cat.' Some admirers say the 'Aby' once romped with the pet lions on the steps of the Imperial Palace in Addis Ababa. Known as the cat from the Blue Nile (Abyssinia is present-day Ethiopia), the Abyssinian is thought by many to be the direct descendant of the sacred cats of ancient Egypt. The mummified remains of some ancient Egyptian cats, possessing the ruddy or red-ticked coloring peculiar to the Abyssinian, and reproductions of them in tombs, were compared with living cats in Abyssinia at the end of the nineteenth century, and an almost perfect similarity between them was discovered. It is known, however, that there were also blue and black cats in ancient Egypt. Both the Egyptian cat and the Abyssinian may well have come from the same wild ancestor, the African Kaffir cat, which is found in both countries.

Although the above is the most widely accepted theory of the origin of the Abyssinian, there are other views. The late Professor HC Brooke, a well known naturalist and authority on cats, believed that the Abyssinian is descended from the African Caracal lynx which, like the yellow African Kaffir cat, has been known to mate with tame cats and can be domesticated if tamed when young. The Caracal lynx shares the ruddy coat color, tufted ears and general appearance of the Abyssinian cat.

Other knowledgeable cat fanciers assert Abyssinians are the result of tabby matings, and that all stories of their Abyssinian and Egyptian ancestry are purely legend. What lends credence to this view is that every now and then kittens of very passable Abyssinian type are born to ordinary tabby parents, and even pedigreed Abyssinians occasionally have kittens with tabby markings, which is heavily penalized in the show ring. These cat authorities believe the Abyssinian is a man-made breed, created by mating carefully selected ticked tabbies of British foundation stock.

The Aby is probably the oldest of the foreign Shorthair cat breeds. Several cats, including one named *Zula*, were taken back to England by soldiers returning from the Abyssinian War in 1868 — thus the origin of its current common name. A female named *Gondar* is recorded in the first Cat Register published in 1898, and by 1905 there was a pair registered in Boston.

These distinctive cats were initially known by an assortment of names as well as Abyssinian, including Hare Cat, Rabbit Cat and Bunny Cat. Their coat is indeed similar to that of the wild hare or rabbit, and in France the normal Aby's coloring (ruddy) is known as *lièvre*, or hare. There exist also blue or cream varieties, but they are very rare and are not accepted in America.

Previous page: **A pair of Himalayans.** *Below and facing page:* **The ancient and lionlike Abyssinian.**

By the 1930s Abyssinian breeders became very active, and today it is not unusual for the Aby to be the largest class of Shorthair cats in competition. This is not surprising, because the Abyssinian is a very elegant and enchanting cat. Its expressive eyes have been described as 'the biggest, most innocent eyes in the world.' They are almond-shaped, come in green, hazel or yellow, and are set in a slightly triangular, delicate, elongated head, crowned by fairly large, sharply-defined ears. Of medium size, the Aby has a svelte, well-muscled and harmoniously proportioned body. It has slender legs, small feet, and a fairly long, tapering tail. Its soft, silky coat is dense and resilient.

The Abyssinian has also been called the 'Little Lion' because of its resemblance to the mountain lion in color and expression. There is a strong strain of wildness in the Aby, and it should therefore be owned by people who can give it plenty of space, for this most feral looking of the domestic breeds loves to climb trees and go hunting. It will pace if penned up. When disturbed, an Aby may move with split-second speed. It loves to leap to high places, such as the top of he refrigerator. Like a lion, it enjoys basking in the sun and moves from window to window. The Aby likes to watch running water and to play with the water in its water dish.

This fearless, friendly and intelligent feline gets along well with dogs and is good with children. It will readily walk with a leash and harness and can be taught to retrieve. The Abyssinian needs to be given special attention by an owner who will indulge and play with it. Otherwise the cat will grow sad, go off by itself and perhaps even run away. Abys often tend to attach themselves to only one person. Men who previously thought they didn't like cats are often attracted to Abyssinians.

The affectionate Abyssinian has a loud purr, but a soft, musical meow, and, when in season, the female is known as a quiet caller. Because Abys are such lively cats, when pregnant the female must be kept inside and watched more than usual to prevent injury. Females may experience rather difficult pregnancies and need help at the time of delivery, when at the most three to four kittens are born. The male, as well as the mother, is gentle with the babies, and lets them bite his tail and clamber on his back.

These pages: **The Abyssinian Cat.**

An Abyssinian kitten *(above)* and a trio of the same *(below)*. *At right:* A full grown Abby. Note the characteristic white on the neck and the black tip on the tail.

AMERICAN SHORTHAIR (DOMESTIC SHORTHAIR)

The American Shorthair's ancestors arrived on the Mayflower with the Pilgrims, having developed from the same stock as the British Shorthair, which apparently arrived in Britain with the Romans. These solid citizens have always been regarded as working cats, for they have never ceased to be good 'mousers,' patrolling barns, warehouses and fields, as well as family homes. It was not until the turn of the century, however, that the first American Shorthairs were registered, and these—an orange tabby male with the distinctly female name *Belle* and a silver tabby called *Pretty Correct*—were British imports! Then, in 1904, *Buster Brown*, a male smoke of unknown American parents, was registered, thus opening the way for the American-bred stock, which were called Domestic Shorthairs until 1966, when the name American Shorthair was adopted. Unpedigreed cats are still called Domestics, and until January of 1985 these non-pedigreed Domestics were accepted by the Cat Fanciers Association (CFA) as foundation stock. To strengthen its roots as a natural American breed, registration associations decided to allow the registration of non-pedigreed cats. In 1971 one such cat was named Best American Shorthair of the Year by the CFA.

The American Shorthair comes in 34 recognized colors and patterns. Most common are: the classic tabby pattern, especially in silver, brown, red, or cameo (fur tipped with red, cream, tabby or tortie instead of black); also common are black, blue, white, calico, shaded silver, or tortoiseshell smoke; mackerel tabby pattern; patched tabby pattern in brown, blue, and silver; classic tabby pattern in blue or cream; dilute calico (blue cream and white, the white predominating on the lower parts); blue-cream; bicolor; van bicolor (red and white, but with a coat pattern very rare in cats: the red color is restricted to areas around the ears and on the tail); van calico; and van blue cream and white. Chocolate, lavender and Himalayan patterns are not allowed.

Males generally weigh about 14 pounds and females ten pounds. They are sturdily built and natural athletes. The American Shorthair's body is medium to large, with heavy shoulders and a well developed chest. It has firm, strong legs of medium length and a medium length tail that ends bluntly. The head is large and well-proportioned with a square muzzle and a firm chin. Slightly rounded, widely set ears frame large, round, slightly slanted eyes that are set well apart.

The American Shorthair is intelligent, affectionate, home-loving and likes children. It attaches itself to every member of the family as long as it is treated with respect and praised when it brings home some little present caught on the run. This gentle and compliant pet, of loud purrs and soft meows, is a great lap cat, if you can bear the weight.

These pages: **The Shaded Silver American Shorthair.**

These pages: **The Silver Tabby American Shorthair.**

AMERICAN WIREHAIR

Adam, the first American Wirehair, was born in an American Shorthair litter in a barn in upstate New York in 1966, and survived a weasel attack which killed his brothers and sisters. The result of a spontaneous mutation, he was adopted by a breeder who started a breeding program.

Because breeders still have little control over the sought-after coat other than seeking to mate the best American Wirehairs to American Shorthairs with thick, densely textured coats, and hoping for the best, since Wirehair to Wirehair crossings do not produce favorable results, there are few American Wirehairs today.

About 50 percent of the kittens born of American Shorthair/American Wirehair matings have curly coats. They look like little lambs, and some with straight coats may have curly coats later, at around eight weeks.

The ideal coat should be of medium length, tightly curled and thick, coarse, resilient and springy to the touch. This medium sized, round and woolly cat comes in the same colors and patterns as the American Shorthair, and resembles that breed in build and personality as well. It is sweet and affectionate and makes a fine pet.

American Wirehairs were accepted for CFA championship in 1978. *(See American Shorthair)*

BALINESE/ JAVANESE

Initially called the 'Longhaired Siamese,' when it appeared as a spontaneous mutation, or recessive genetic characteristic, in litters of certain Siamese bloodlines, and then named 'Balinese' because its graceful movements resemble those of Balinese dancers, this slim, dainty cat has the same long, flowing lines and deep blue eyes as the Siamese. Its coat is not so heavy as other longhaired breeds, and it has no ruff, but it is soft and silky, and the tail is like a plume.

While the Balinese comes in all the colors of the Siamese rainbow, the CFA recognizes just the four basic colors — seal, chocolate, blue, and lilac — for championship status. Other associations also accept the red, tortie and lynx-point patterns, but the CFA dubs these 'Javanese' and accepts them for registration but not for championship.

American cat fanciers soon discovered that by mating a pair of the longhaired cats a litter of identical longhaired kittens resulted, and the breed was on its way. First recognized in 1963 in the United States, by 1970 the Balinese was being shown in Europe.

Like the Siamese, the Balinese/Javanese love attention, are bright, lively, playful, and persistent, yet are quieter than the Siamese in voice and temperament. Because their coats do not mat and snarl, Balinese and Javanese are easy to groom. All in all, with their alert, engaging personalities, svelte dancers' bodies, and easy-care, long, silky fur, Balinese and Javanese make lovely pets.

Right: **Except for its long-flowing coat, the Balinese has many characteristics in common with the Siamese.**

BIRMAN

According to legend, the Birman, also called the Sacred Cat of Burma, guarded the temples in that country in ancient times. In the Temple of Lao-Tsun, where a golden goddess with blue eyes, Tsun-Kyan-Kse, was worshipped, the priests lived with their sacred cats. One day the temple was attacked by raiders who killed the head priest while he was meditating before the goddess. By his side was his pure white cat, *Sinh*, his faithful companion, who put his paws on the body of his dead master, defying the enemy raiders. As he did this, his body fur turned golden, the color of the goddess, while his paws remained white, symbolic of purity. His legs, face, ears and tail became earth-colored, and his yellow eyes turned a sapphire blue.

Sinh remained in front of the goddess for seven days, refusing all food. Then he died, taking with him the old priest's soul to Paradise. When the priests met to choose a successor to the head priest, the hundred white cats of the temple came slowly into the main hall, and to the amazement of all assembled, they were no longer white, but had taken on the same coloring as that of the dead *Sinh*. They formed a circle around one young priest, Ligoa, who was chosen as the new head priest.

Whatever its origin, this extremely beautiful, longhaired cat was first described by a major in the British Army in 1898, but was not established as a breed until 1925 in France. Birmans really became known around the time of the Second World War, when they appeared at a number of cat shows in Europe. In Britain, recognition was granted by the Governing Council of the Cat Fancy in 1966; the cat was recognized by the CFA in the United States in 1967.

The American standard calls for a medium-to large sized cat with a broad, round head; strong bones; a straight nose; full cheeks; a firm mouth; thick whiskers; a long, massive body, supported on medium-length, strong legs and short, strong paws; with a bushy tail; and a ruff. The body fur is long, silky and creamy golden, and comes in a variety of points (the mask — ears, legs and tail — of a darker color), and pure white gloves on all four feet. Ideally these gauntlets should match in size and shape. The points may be seal, a definite dark brown; blue, a blue-gray; lilac, a lilac-gray color; and/or chocolate, milk chocolate. All Birmans have almost round, slightly slanted, brilliant blue eyes, which have been described as 'fascinating.'

There is an American variety of shorthaired Birman called the Snowshoe Cat, or Silverlace, because of its white paws, which is not generally recognized as yet.

Similar to other Oriental cats, Birmans are very sexy. When the female comes in season (between five and seven months old the first time), she announces her desires by calling loudly and rubbing vigorously against her owner and the furniture. She is willing to mate frequently and with fervor, and kittens easily, perhaps owing to her longer body. The kittens, of which there are usually four, are born with light-colored, solid coats, but the dark markings appear after a few months.

Birmans are intelligent, friendly and affectionate, and speak in a sweet, well-behaved voice. They keep themselves very clean and their coats are easy to care for. Because they are basically quiet-natured, they prefer a tranquil environment. They live happily in an apartment, but enjoy a promenade on the terrace or in the garden in fair weather.

These pages: **The Birman Cat.**

Above: The long, silky hair of the enchanting Birman is surprisingly easy to care for. The texture of the hair prevents mats if the cat is brushed on a regular basis.

BOMBAY

Owing to its special coloring, the Bombay is known as 'the patent leather kid with the new penny eyes.' Despite its name, this unique, shorthaired, glossy black cat with bright, coppery eyes is an American breed, which was created in 1958 by successful crossings between the Burmese and the American Shorthair. Because the Bombay resembles the black leopard of India, it was named for the city of Bombay. It has also been referred to as a mini-panther. The Cat Fanciers Association (CFA) accepted the breed for championship in 1976.

This charming cat is contented in an apartment. It is a good companion, quiet, sensitive, affectionate, reserved, intelligent and soft-voiced, but it can also be impish and sometimes silly. Its pet hate is loud noises.

Bombays are medium-sized, muscular and surprisingly heavy for their size. They have rounded heads, chubby faces and rounded ears which perk up at the slightest noise. The tail is elegant and of intermediate length.

There are four to five light-colored kittens in a litter, which become totally black by the sixth month.

Facing page: **Even though its green eyes are considered a fault by** *show* **standards, this Bombay is a beautiful animal.** *This page:* **The Bombay.**

BRITISH SHORTHAIR

The British Shorthairs of today are the descendants of domestic cats brought to Britain by Caesar and the conquering Roman legions. (Their counterparts are the European Shorthair and the American Shorthair.) During the 400 years that the Romans ruled Britain these house cats doubtless mated with the local European wildcats, but careful breeding since the nineteenth century has produced short-haired cats which conform to a set standard.

Ideal British Shorthairs can be described as 'square,' with short, firm, and dense fur. Their bodies should be short and sturdy, and their legs short and strong, with a short, thick tail, rounded at the tip. The head should be massive and rounded, with the ears and eyes set wide apart, over full cheeks, a short, straight nose, and a firm chin, rising from a short, round neck. Big, round, open, even eyes reveal that this is an animal with inner strength that can handle most any situation.

Harrison Weir, who wrote the first comprehensive book on cats in 1889, in which the British Shorthair was given the most prominent place, so loved the British street cat that he almost single-handedly elevated it to a registerable breed. Until the turn of the century, the British Shorthair was the most popular cat in the cat shows held at the Crystal Palace in London. Then the exotic Persians and Siamese landed on England's shores, capturing people's fancies, and it was

not until the 1930s that the British Shorthair again regained popularity. They lost ground, as did all breeds, during the Second World War. After the war, there were so few pedigreed Shorthair studs left that breeders, to perpetuate the breed, crossed British Shorthairs with Siamese and Persians, succeeding only in creating cats that were too lanky or cats that were too woolly. Conscientious selective breeding programs finally brought the British Shorthair back to its desired square shape, with short, firm, and dense coat.

There are now 18 recognized colors and patterns. The British Blue is one of the most popular shorthaired cats in the United Kingdom. Its coat is light to medium blue, with blue nose leather and paw pads and copper or orange eyes.

These pages: **The Orange-eyed British White.**

There are three variations of British White: blue-eyed, orange- or yellow-eyed, and odd-eyed. Blue-eyed whites are rare and, though very beautiful, are usually deaf. Those with orange eyes are handsome and occasionally deaf. Odd-eyed whites are rare and useful in breeding programs.

White cats, in times past, were said to possess magical powers and to bring good luck to their owners. In fairy tales, the white cat might be the handsome prince or the beautiful princess in disguise.

British Blacks with orange eyes are particularly striking, and suggest Shakespeare's lines in *Pericles*, 'the cat with eye of burning coal that crouches near the mouse's hole.' Sir Winston Churchill's superb British Black, *Nelson*, followed him around and slept on his bed.

In the Middle Ages, black cats were thought to be unlucky and became the unfortunate recipients of hatred and cruelty as superstitions swirled around them. They were said to be companions of Satan and witches. Because black cats seem to have more electricity in their fur than cats of other colors, which causes it to crackle when touched in frosty weather, ignorant people, no doubt, began to fear them.

The British Shorthair Tabby comes in a variety of colors: silver, red, brown, cream, and blue. Mackerel Tabbies' coats resemble the fish of that name. It is believed that all domestic cats once had tabby markings, and, if all the domestic cats in the world were allowed to mate freely, there only would be tabby cats left.

According to the dictionary, the word 'tabby' comes from a type of ribbed silk or taffeta which was developed in an area of old Baghdad known as Attabiya.

British Tortoiseshell and Tortoiseshell and White Shorthairs are most often female because sex and color are genetically linked. The few males which are born are generally infertile. In the United States, Tortoiseshell and White Shorthairs are called Calico cats.

British Bicolored Shorthairs, of which the black and white variety were known as Magpie cats, were exhibited in the Any Other Variety classes until 1966, when they were granted their own breed number and championship status. The original standard, which called for the Bicolor to be marked exactly like a Dutch rabbit, with the mask being precisely divided down the middle by color, proved too difficult to emulate, and the standard was amended to require only that the patches be clear and evenly distributed, with not more than two-thirds of the coat to be colored and not more than one-half of the coat to be white. Spotted, shaded and tipped varieties, in rainbow hues, have become popular in recent years.

All British Shorthairs, of whatever color or pattern, are quiet, gentle and affectionate pets. They are also known for being brave and able to take care of themselves. There are many stories of British Shorthairs that warned their owners of impending danger and of mother cats fiercely defending their young.

British Shorthairs occur in various colors — white *(facing page)*, **blue** *(above and below)* **and black** *(below)*.

CHOOSING YOUR CAT

Choosing a cat can be as easy as feeding the local stray or as difficult as buying a pedigreed, show-quality kitten.

A main consideration in selecting a cat is the family it will be entering. It is not recommended that a kitten be introduced into a family with small children. It is easier to accustom a dog to the new member of the family than to teach toddlers not to crush the cat! In this instance, an adult cat is a better choice. It will determine how much man-handling it will tolerate very quickly. (A supply of soap, water and Band-Aids may be necessary if the child is stubborn about 'loving' the cat.)

On the other hand, a kitten will easily adjust to older children and adults. If the family already has other cats, dogs, birds or other pets, a kitten is definitely the best choice. The other pets will still defend their territory, but a kitten is a lesser threat than another adult. As long as the kitten is very slowly introduced to the other pets and never left alone with them until the entire family has adjusted to the idea of a new member, everything will work out fine. The most incorrigible dog will eventually accept a kitten. It may take some time and patience, but it will work if the owner is determined.

The decision as to whether to take in a house cat or buy a registered cat can be a difficult one. Each has advantages and disadvantages. An ordinary house cat is inexpensive. Nearly everyone has a neighbor who will be happy to provide a kitten. The Humane Society or the pound may also have cats and kittens for a minimal fee. Unfortunately, however, the kitten may also have parasites, viruses or congenital defects.

The registered kitten is much more expensive but the owner will know what he is getting. Both parents are known, with all

Above: **A kitten (or two, as seen** *at right***) can more easily adapt to a new family with children and other pets than can an older cat. This full-grown cat** *(below)* **does not take kindly to the pet rabbit in his yard.**

the qualities of the particular breed easily observable. The cats are bred for certain traits which are known to the breeder. The ancestry of the animal can be traced back for generations.

One important recommendation for the future of the cat concerns neutering. Many people hold the mistaken notion that neutering is cruel to the animal. Nothing could be farther from the truth. The neutered cat is a happier animal. It does not howl when in heat, nor does it roam the neighborhood fighting other cats. In addition, male cats often develop the habit of spraying their pungent urine to mark their territory. If neutered early, this habit will not develop, thus sparing the owner many hours of attempting to eradicate the strong odor that will fill the home.

Today, many veterinarians recommend that, unless the cat is registered and the owner plans to breed it, the cat should be neutered before breeding. There are already too many unwanted animals roaming the cities and countryside. Anyone who has had the unhappy experience of attempting to give away a litter of kittens can testify to the difficulty in finding good homes for their pets. In addition, a neutered animal does not become fat or sluggish unless the owner feels guilty and overfeeds it. It will have a better disposition and will be a more loving member of the family.

In any case, the owner should always follow his instincts in choosing the newest addition to his family. A playful, curious, healthy kitten is one of the best pets that anyone can have.

Facing page: **A pet door lets this cat come and go as she pleases.** *Above:* **Two friends engage in some good-natured roughhousing.** *Below:* **A house cat on her favorite perch.**

BURMESE

A brown Burmese looks like polished mahogany and has a friendly, playful personality. Such charms as these so captivated Dr Joseph Thompson, a United States Navy psychiatrist, that in 1930 he brought a little brown female cat from Rangoon, named *Wong Mau*, home with him to San Francisco, and started the first pedigreed breed to be developed completely in the United States.

Because there were no similar cats available with which to mate Wong Mau, Dr Thompson arranged matings with her closest cousin, a Siamese, followed by crosses between the offspring and back to *Wong Mau*.

All *Wong Mau*'s kittens were hybrids, but when mated back to their mother brown kittens resembling their mother were produced. Thus began the Burmese dynasty. Nearly all modern, pedigreed Burmese can trace their ancestry back to *Wong Mau*.

During the 1930s and early 1940s Dr Thompson and other American breeders, in the process of developing the breed, imported a few more Burmese from Burma so that the inbreeding could be reduced, and some outcrossings to Siamese were also carried out.

The Burmese was first officially recognized by the CFA in 1936 and by the Governing Council of the Cat Fancy (GCCF), which in Britain is the group responsible for registering purebred cats in that country, in 1952; the breed is now well established in Europe, as well as in Australia and New Zealand.

These pages: **The Burmese Cat.**

Of medium size, the Burmese is long, graceful and elegant, but also muscular. It has a long neck, round chest, slender legs, and well-shaped, oval feet. The head is rounded on top between the ears, which are rounded at the tips and set wide apart, and the eyes are large, rounded, of a golden yellow color, wide-set, and very expressive. Below the lustrous eyes there is a shorter muzzle than that of the Siamese, a pronounced chin, and a strong jaw. The tail is long and straight, tapering at the tip.

Burmese in America are more rounded and less foreign in head shape than those in Europe and elsewhere. The American breed standard states that the head should be 'pleasingly rounded, without flat planes, whether viewed from front or side.'

Cats resembling the Burmese are illustrated in *The Cat Book Poems* of 1350 AD, and these drawings may be of ancestors of Havana Browns, but almost certainly capture early examples of Burmese. Brown cats appeared at 19th century cat shows and could well have been early Burmese or Burmese-Siamese hybrids.

The short, dense and glossy coat is a marked feature in all Burmese. All cat fancy organizations agree that brown, or sable, as it's called in North America, is the primary color of the breed, and this is the only color recognized as Burmese in the United States. Great Britain, however, additionally recognizes red, cream, blue, lilac, chocolate, brown tortie, blue tortie, chocolate tortie and lilac tortie. *(See Malayan)*

Burmese of whatever color have a delightful sense of humor and are capable of laughing at themselves, an indication of their intelligence and sweet disposition. They are happy, active cats with softer voices than Siamese and make excellent companions.

Male Burmese perform a dance with their hind legs called the 'Burmese shuffle' before pouncing or prior to spraying. Females are precocious, starting calling at about five months. They have litters of about six kittens, which become playful at about six weeks.

Only the sable Burmese, like the cats on *these pages*, is recognized by the American CFA. The British recognize a wider variety of colors. *Below:* A Burmese (right) and his Siamese cousin (left).

The Burmese *(left and below)* was influenced by the Siamese and has inherited the Siamese personality and muscular body, but has a rounder head and smaller ears than the Siamese.

CHARTREUX

Although the origin of the Chartreux is mysterious, it is certainly French, and most cat fanciers agree with the theory that the Carthusian monks, famous for their Chartreuse liqueur, were also responsible for creating the Chartreux cat.

Just when the cat was first bred at la grande Chartreuse monastery, near Grenoble, is unknown, but the French poet du Bellay celebrated the Chartreux as a formidable ratter as early as 1558, and by the eighteenth century the naturalists Linnaeus and de Buffon recognized the Chartreux as a distinct breed. During the 1930s a French veterinarian bestowed a Latin name on the breed: *Felix catus carthusianorum*. And the French novelist Collette wrote of her own cat: 'The sun played on her Chartreux coat, mauve and blue like a wood pigeon's neck.'

Some Chartreux were brought to the United States around 1970, and enough cats were produced to gain the breed recognition by several associations. Although the cat has not been recognized for show by the Cat Fanciers Association, it may be registered.

Today, few true Chartreux remain in France. (Their numbers were especially decimated during World War II.) Most have some Persian or British Blue blood — or both — and since 1973 the British and French versions have been officially judged by the same standard, as over the years the differences between the two have all but disappeared. There are, however, some North American Associations that place Chartreux in a separate class and judge them by their own point standard.

This big, blue cat has a broad chest and powerful hind legs, and a large head with wide forehead, extremely full cheeks, and narrow, but not pointed, muzzle. Its eyes are round and shaded from gold to copper; they express the cat's sweet nature and trust. The Chartreux has strong jaws and appears to be smiling. A sour-faced cat is penalized in the show ring.

Males weigh between ten and 14 pounds and females between six and nine pounds. Although similar to a British Blue, the French cat has a broad head, whereas the Brit's is round. Silvery highlights on the fur of the Chartreux are especially prized, while all hues of blue are equally popular on the British cat. The fur should be dense, plush, of intermediate length, and as soft as bunny fur.

This good-sized hunter needs room to move around, so adapts best to a place with a terrace or a garden. While it can be rough on rodents, it knows its strength and is gentle with people. It loves children and large dogs, and, in fact, everyone who treats it with respect and love.

- Chartreux have an average of two kittens per litter. They are roly-poly, sturdy and slow to wean, eating everything in sight while continuing to nurse for at least two months.

These pages: **The Chartreux Cat.**

Some authorities consider the Chartreux to be the same breed as the British Blue. You be the judge—compare the cats on *these pages* with the Blues on *page 37*.

CORNISH REX — *see Rex*

CYMRIC

The Cymric (pronounced kim'rik), got its name, which is the Celtic word for Welsh, because the Isle of Man (origin of the Manx) is in the Irish Sea, halfway between Ireland and Wales. *(See Manx)*

The Cymric is a longhaired Manx, and must abide by the same show requirements as the Manx — the most important feature being a complete absence of tail. Its long fur is the result of a recessive gene, and mating two Cymrics produces 100 percent Cymric kittens. However, since tailless cats carry a lethal factor when mated together too often, tailed or stumpy-tailed cats should be introduced into the breeding program from time to time.

Cymrics first occurred in Manx litters in Canada in the 1960s and are still confined to the North American show ring. Full championship status is pending.

Like the Manx, the Cymric *(these pages)* **is tailless, and has short front legs, longer hind legs and a short back.**

DEVON REX — *see Rex*

EGYPTIAN MAU

The Egyptian Mau may be the first domestic cat. A wall painting from a temple at Thebes, of about 1400 BC, shows a spotted cat on a duck-hunting expedition, and a papyrus, of about 1100 BC, shows the sun-god, Ra, in the form of a spotted cat. 'Mau' means 'cat' and 'sun' in the ancient Egyptian language. It also represents the sound cats make.

In the religion of ancient Egypt, many of the gods were identified with certain animals, such as the hawk, jackal, lion, or bull, but the most visible animal was the cat. It was closely identified with both Ra, the sun god, and Pasht, the moon goddess. Statues of these gods depicted them as men or women with the heads of those animals with which they were identified. Pasht was Ra's consort and closest companion: while Ra made the daylight, Pasht made the moonlight. For many of her activities, Pasht transformed herself into a cat, so it was possible that any stray cat could be the goddess. The people, therefore, regarded all cats as sacred, and causing the death of a cat, even unintentionally, was punishable by death. Herodotus, in his *History*, relates it was a greater crime to kill a cat than to murder a man, and if a house caught fire, the cats were saved before the humans. Every household had cats, because they were thought to protect against misfortune. If a cat died, the family went into deep mourning and all members shaved off their eyebrows to express their sorrow. The mummified body of the beloved pet was placed in an

This silver Egyptian Mau *(pages 54–57)* **shows the characteristic spots, facial markings and long tail, tipped in black.**

ornate mummy case, along with bowls of milk and mummified mice, and buried with solemn rites in a cat cemetery.

As the leadership of Egypt in the ancient world gradually declined under the onslaughts of foreign invaders, the gods and goddesses of Egypt lost their power and were replaced, in the fourth century AD, during the reign of Constantine, by the Christian religion with its angels and saints.

Over the years, Egyptian Maus lived their normal cat lives, in homes or in the streets in Egypt, and today they are the only natural spotted, Oriental-type domestic cats.

The modern Egyptian Mau dates to 1953, when Princess Natalie Troubetskoye imported a female to Italy and crossed her with another Egyptian Mau, which union produced two kittens. The male kitten was subsequently bred back to his mother and the breed began. Princess Troubetskoye brought a pair of Maus to America, and they were shown at the Empire Cat Show in London, England in 1957.

The breed was not recognized until 15 years later by the Cat Fanciers Association (CFA). Now, all the North American associations recognize it as a championship breed, though the Governing Council of the Cat Fancy in Britain does not.

Similar in build to the Abyssinian, which has also been compared to the ancient Egyptian cats, the Egyptian Mau is medium sized, with a wedge-shaped head, and a graceful, well-muscled body, set on long legs, the back longer than the front legs. The ideal Mau has an 'M,'or scarab, on its forehead and frown marks (the M-shaped marks on the foreheads of tabby cats), and its cheeks are decorated with mascara lines, one of which also extends horizontally around the sides of the head after originating from the outside corner of each eye. Its body is randomly spotted; and its tail is ringed with a dark tip. The fur is dense, resilient and silky, and comes in three recognized colors: silver (black spots on a silver agouti* background), bronze (chocolate spots on bronze agouti) and smoke (black spots on gray, with a silver undercoat). Pale gooseberry-green eyes are preferred with all fur colors.

Egyptian Maus can be somewhat aloof with strangers, for they make friends only with the people they like. Depending on the bloodlines and rearing environment, Maus may enjoy being handled and shown or dislike it and react adversely. Most are intelligent, docile pets, patient with children and very affectionate. They are known for their good memories.

Both parents take care of the kittens, which are sturdy and develop slowly. The kittens' eyes get greener when they are happy, but turn amber if they are upset.

*Agouti is an irregularly barred pattern of fur.

EXOTIC SHORTHAIR

This cat was created by American breeders to fulfill the fantasy of cat fanciers who are partial to Persians but don't want to be bothered with the long, flowing coat.

The breed was developed in the 1960s by crossing Persians with American Shorthairs. At first, Burmese and British Shorthairs were also used for breeding, but since 1968 these two types have not been allowed.

The Exotic Shorthair is the only hybrid cross allowed today in the United States. To be registered as an Exotic Shorthair, a cat must have one Persian parent and one American Shorthair parent, two Exotic Shorthair parents or one Persian and one Exotic Shorthair parent.

Originally, all the shorthaired cats in America (except for those of foreign type, such as the Abyssinian and Siamese breeds) were considered as one class, then known as Domestic, but now known as the American Shorthair. Judges at shows unfailingly chose the cats with shorter noses and smaller ears and breeders crossed more and more Domestics with Persians in order to produce cats with those winning characteristics. They became very popular, but the breeders of American Shorthairs who preferred to stick with crossing American Shorthairs to American Shorthairs were disgruntled, since they seldom, if ever, won any prizes.

It was suggested that there be two classes for Domestic cats and two standards, one for the American Shorthair and one for the Exotic Shorthair. The Cat Fanciers Association did indeed eventually adopt this suggestion. Earlier American Shorthairs, similar to the Exotic in type, were allowed to be re-registered as Exotics and to keep any ribbons they had won as American Shorthairs.

The show requirements for the Exotic Shorthair are the same as those set for the Persian, but the coat should be 'dense, plush and soft in texture, full of life. It stands out from the body due to density, is not flat or close-lying, and is medium in length, slightly longer than other shorthairs, but not long enough to flow.' An even coat is an absolute requirement, and judges take off points for feathery hair on the ears or tail, or any tufting between the toes. A delicate head, or a short or kinked tail will also lower the score. All colors and patterns of the American Shorthair and Persian are allowed.

This is a healthy, intelligent, gentle, affectionate cat, which is contented in an apartment. It might jump as high as the bed to get comfortable.

The Exotic Shorthair comes in a wide range of colors, including the Cream Tabby *below* **and the Brown Tabby on the** *facing page*.

Above: A Mackerel Tabby Exotic Shorthair. Note the large, round head; the full, wide-set eyes and the short, snub nose.

Below: **A champion Exotic Shorthair lounging among his prize-winning ribbons.**

SANTA CLARA
VALLEY CAT
FANCIERS

April 22, 1984

ALLBREED

Mary
Kilborn

HAVANA BROWN

This mahogany-colored cat got its name from the Havana cigar or the Havana rabbit, both of which it resembles in color.

All-brown cats have been treasured for years. Their beauty was celebrated by the poets of ancient Siam, and they were said to protect their owners from all evil. They arrived early in the West; the earliest example is a cat exhibited in the late 1800s as the 'Swiss Mountain Cat.' Then in 1930 a solid brown feline appeared in the category 'Brown Cat.'

To achieve the rich, warm burnt sienna desired on a consistent basis, two breeders in Britain began experimenting in the early 1950s and finally came up with the right formula. By crossing a seal point Siamese, carrying the chocolate brown gene, with a shorthaired, black queen, they created the first kitten of the new color in 1952, and it was exhibited for the first time in 1953.

Some years passed and British breeders, working to produce the perfect brown cat, crossed Russian Blues, Siamese and shorthairs of mixed ancestry, arriving at the Havana Brown as we know it today, although its conformation differs somewhat between England and the United States. In Britain a Siamesé-type body is preferred, whereas Americans prefer the earlier, moderately foreign, type. The standard for judging Havanas follows that for Russian Blues.

This breed of cat was recognized by the Governing Council of the Cat Fancy in Britain in 1958 under the name Chestnut Brown Foreign, which was subsequently changed to Havana; and by the Cat Fanciers Association, in America, in 1959, as the Havana Brown.

These medium-sized cats, with rosy-brown nose leather, rosy-pink-brown paw pads, brown whiskers, and vivid green eyes have a distinctive rectangular muzzle, with a break on either side of the whisker pads, which makes the jowls seem wider, followed by a strong chin. There is a definite stop (an indentation between the forehead and the nose) at the eyes, and the very large ears, pricked slightly forward, give the cat an alert look. The cat's long legs make it appear tall for its length, but its tail is in proportion to its body.

This sleek, beautiful cat has lots of personality. It often has the unusual habit of using its paws to investigate strange objects by touch, instead of relying on its sense of smell, as do other breeds. Shoulders are its favorite perch and it will raise its paw to greet people. The Havana loves to play with cardboard boxes and paper bags and enjoys the company of other cats. It's a fine apartment cat, but likes a small terrace.

Havana kittens look like bats because of their large ears and pink noses, and the mother tends to talk constantly with them. These intelligent and very active babies are out of the box by three weeks and respond to the human voice before they open their eyes. The males are chauvinists, leaving the kitten rearing to the queen.

These pages: **The Havana Brown.**

These pages: **The Havana Brown.**

HIMALAYAN

The creation of the 'Himmy,' which is a Persian-type cat with a long, flowing coat and a Siamese pattern, took years of selective breeding, for these cats are completely opposite: the Persian is short, stocky and heavy-boned, with long fur, whereas the Siamese is long, slim, and fine-boned, with short fur.

A Swedish geneticist started the process in 1924 by crossing Siamese, Birman, and Persian cats. His results were apparently inconclusive, for in the 1930s two Harvard Medical School workers continued working on the project. They crossed Siamese with Smoke, Silver Tabby, and Black Persians, and a large number of shorthaired kittens were produced. Then they mated two of these kittens and a longhaired, black female was born. When bred to her father, she gave birth to *Debutante*, the first Himalayan, with points and long hair. It had taken five years to come up with *Debutante*. The year was 1935, the same year that an experimental breeders' club was started in Britain with the idea of making similar matings. As the Harvard workers had only wanted to increase their knowledge of genetics, and had no interest in establishing a new breed, they considered their project completed.

The British experimental breeders found Debutante to be too Siamese-like in shape, so they carried on with more matings. Then, in 1947, a lady asked one of the breeders if he would accept her longhaired, Siamese-patterned female, of unknown pedigree, into their breeding program. The breeder later wrote: 'When I saw this queen I was astonished at her beauty. Apart from her coloring she possessed no Siamese characteristics and was reasonably Persian in type.' This lovely feline became an important part of the British breeding program over the next eight years.

Meanwhile, other American breeders were attempting to produce a Persian with points, and it is thought they were responsible for the name 'Himalayan,' after the Himalayan rabbit, which has similar

These pages: **Himalayan Kittens.**

These pages: **The Himalayan Cat.**

coloring. It was not until the 1950s, however, that Himalayan breeding began in earnest in the United States, when several breeders were working toward creating the just-right plump and pointed cat.

In England, with the Governing Council of the Cat Fancy requiring three generations of like-to-like matings, hundreds of cats and in-breedings were involved before recognition was achieved in 1955. Within three years a Colourpoint (as they are called in England) kitten won a prize for being the best longhaired kitten at the 1958 Kensington Kitten and Neuter Cat Club Show. Yet the British breeders realized further outcrosses were necessary to improve type and coat, and ten more years went by before they were fully pleased they had attained their goal.

Cautious American breeders, not wanting to present their creation to the public until perfection, or near perfection, had been achieved, held off exhibiting until 1957, when the first two examples of the new breed were shown at a San Diego cat show. They dazzled the crowd and the judges. The American Cat Fanciers Association and the Cat Fanciers Association both voted to recognize the new breed that same year. By 1961 all the major American associations recognized the Himalayan.

Originally available in only two colors, seal point and blue point, Himalayans now come in chocolate point, lilac point, red (flame) point, tortie point (all colors), and lynx (tabby) point (all colors). Some American associations recognize more colors than others. British cat fanciers accept all of the above colors, plus cream point,

and breeders on both sides of the Atlantic are working toward the creation of more beautiful color patterns. Himalayans generally combine the temperaments of their forebears. They are more enterprising than most Persians, liking to choose their own activities, yet are good natured, affectionate, and gentle, rarely showing the capricious character of the Siamese. Their voices are usually louder than that of a Persian, but quieter than those of their Siamese ancestors.

Females may call as early as eight months, earlier than most Persians, perhaps revealing the Siamese genes, but males are not normally ready to sire until they are a year and a half old.

Kittens are born white, with pink paw pads, noses, and ears, and only at six months are the markings established.

At maturity, the ideal show cat has fur five inches long. Although judges require dark points and light body color, the long fur prevents Himalayans from becoming as dense at the points as the Siamese because the Siamese pattern is controlled by the temperature, and the fluffy, longer fur traps more warm air than the smooth, short hair of the Siamese. The pale body color is easier to obtain than in the Siamese. All Himmies have deep blue eyes.

While breeders were developing chocolate point and lilac point Himalayans, solid chocolate and solid lilac cats sometimes resulted. These solid-color Himalayans are called 'Kashmirs' in some associations; the CFA considers them to be a division of the Persian. Kashmirs fit into the Longhair category in Great Britain.

Himalayans were developed because cat fanciers desired a cat with the thick coat of a Persian and the coloring of a Siamese. The long, glossy coat of this Blue Point Himalayan (below) is typical of this beautiful breed.

In the process of developing the Himalayan, two solid colors resulted — the lilac *(above)* and the chocolate *(right)* — when Chocolate Point Siamese and Havanas were introduced into the bloodline.

JAPANESE BOBTAIL

Japanese traditionally regard Japanese Bobtail cats as lucky, and replicas of these *mi-ke* (mee-kay, meaning three colors) cats, with right paw raised in greeting, are a symbol of welcome and good luck.

While this popular domestic cat has existed in Japan for centuries, and is first mentioned in a manuscript written by a tutor to the Empress 1000 years ago, it originally came from China and Korea. A familiar figure in Japanese art, it is seen in ancient prints and paintings and is shown on the front of the Gotokuji Temple in Tokyo, with upraised paw to symbolize good fortune.

It is said that the first cats to step on Japanese soil were black, and that they were then followed by white ones, and then orange cats arrived — and thus the three-colored fur came to be.

An American cat lover living in Japan, who adopted many mi-ke cats, and especially tried to breed the tri-colored ones, sent the first three Bobtail Cats to the United States after the Second World War. Later, when she returned, she took 38 cats with her.

Japanese interest in the breed grew only after American judges visiting a Japanese cat show in 1963 praised the Bobtails. They were recognized by the CFA in 1978, but the breed is still rare in the United States, and is not yet recognized in Europe.

This unique cat with the multi-kinked tail has particularly high cheekbones, slanted, luminous eyes, and large, upright ears, set at a
continued on page 81

These pages and overleaf: **The Japanese Bobtail.**

These pages: **Japanese Bobtail Kittens.**

continued from page 76
pronounced slant, all part of a head which forms an almost perfect equilateral triangle. All of these elements combine to give its face a distinctly Japanese look. The bobbed tail, which is the outstanding characteristic of the breed, is about four inches long and more thickly furred than the rest of the cat, giving it a pom-pom appearance. It is carried erect. Straight, stub tails are unacceptable for show. Japanese Bobtails are medium size to large and have well-muscled, yet lean and straight, bodies. Their hind legs are longer than their front legs, but are deeply angulated so that the standing cat appears to be level. It has a silky, medium-length coat and comes in a variety of colors.

In fact, any color is acceptable except for Siamese-pattern or Abyssinian-type agouti.

Bobs make ideal family pets, for they are affectionate, intelligent, lively, and good mousers, with quiet voices. They particularly like to eat fish.

The kittens are inordinately large at birth, especially the heads and feet. Generally healthy, they are vigorous and soon pouncing on each other and playing at hunting.

Although similar to Manx cats, Japanese Bobtail Cats are not related to them because their tails are due to a recessive gene and breed true, whereas the Manx's lack of a tail is a genetic defect.

KORAT

With its heart-shaped face, large, luminous green eyes, graceful, rounded body, and glossy, silver-blue coat, it is easy to see why the Korat (pronounced koh-raht) has been valued for centuries in its native Thailand.

Originally, these cats could be obtained only as a gift from one owner to another, and it was once the custom to give a Korat to princes and other dignitaries as a sign of devotion. Today the Korat is rare even in Thailand, and ownership is restricted by the government.

The Korat is one of the first cats mentioned in history, and today's Korat is identical to the ancient one as depicted in *The Cat Book Poems*, written between AD 1350 and 1767, and preserved in

Bangkok's National Library. It has the same semi-cobby body, large, curved ears, big, alert, oval eyes, and silver-tipped coat.

A Thai poet wrote in the above-mentioned manuscript about the Korat, 'whose hairs are smooth with roots like clouds and tips like silver,' and whose 'eyes shine like dewdrops on a lotus leaf.' In addition to being appreciated for their beauty, Korats are reputed to bring good luck, being pictured in the ancient manuscript as one of 17 types of good luck cats.

Korats come from the province of Korat in Thailand (which used to be Siam), but in their own country they are called 'Si-Siwat,' because their silver-blue fur resembles the seed of a fruit plant by that name.

The Korat probably first appeared at a National Cat Club Show in England in 1896, when a blue cat entered in the Siamese class was disqualified as being 'blue instead of biscuit-color.' Its owner protested that the cat certainly came from Siam and there were many more like it there. The first record of registration in the United States

These pages: **The Korat.**

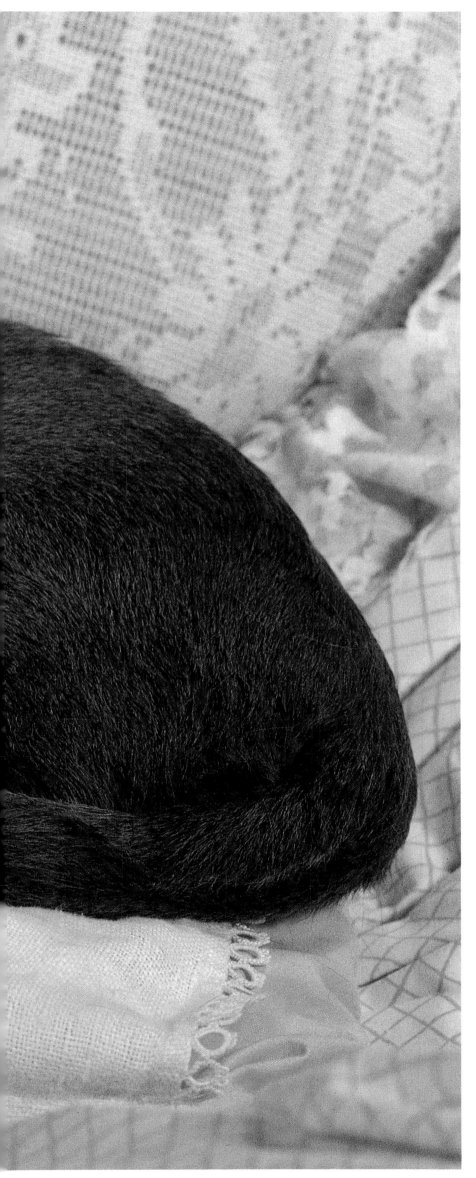

Left and above: **Today the gentle Korat is rare even in its native Thailand.**

dates from 1959, when two Korats, named *Nara* and *Darra*, arrived in Oregon. The Korat Cat Fanciers Association was founded in 1965 to protect the purity of Korat bloodlines and to ensure that only those cats with Thai ancestry are registered. These good luck cats were accepted for CFA championship status in 1966, and by 1969 they were also recognized in Australia and South Africa. It took till 1975 for them to be recognized in Great Britain, and then without championship status, because there was opposition at first from cat fanciers who felt that they were not different enough from other recognized blue shorthairs.

Korats, in general, are gentle, intelligent cats who speak with a soft voice. They have a sense of responsibility to the family and have been known to alert them in emergencies. Although the Korat enjoys the close companionship of its owner and is good with children, it is reticent with strangers and intolerant of strange cats in the house. In fact, the males can be extremely aggressive and have a reputation as street fighters in Thailand. It is, therefore, important to find a breeder who is selective about temperament traits, as well as health and beauty. Korats are profoundly aware of everything around them and do not like to be startled by sudden noises. As a consequence, they may be nervous at shows.

The kittens and adult cats are especially prone to upper-respiratory viruses, so routine vaccinations are important. Both female and male lovingly care for the kittens, which go through an 'ugly duckling' stage, and do not reach their full beauty until they are about two years old. Females remain playful at an advanced age.

MAINE COON CAT

A popular legend holds that the Maine Coon Cat originated from matings between semi-wild domestic cats and raccoons. This idea is supported by the Maine Coon Cat's usual coloring (raccoon-like dark tabby) and its bushy tail. This is how the cat got its name, but it is, of course, biologically impossible.

There are other theories as to the origin of the Maine Coon, but what is a definite fact is that this is one of the oldest natural breeds of North America and is generally regarded as a native of the state of Maine.

Another story states that Marie Antoinette, when planning to escape at the time of the French Revolution, sent her cats to be cared for in the United States until she could be reunited with them.

Still another possibility is that Leif the Lucky brought a Norwegian Forest Cat with him when he landed in the New England region five centuries before Columbus, and the cat missed the boat

These pages: **The Maine Coon Cat.**

Above and right: **The Maine Coon is an intelligent and gentle house pet.**

when the Norsemen sailed for home. The 'Norsk Skaukatt' is very similar to the Maine Coon, differing only in that its hind legs are slightly longer than its front legs and it always has a double coat. The latter characteristic does sometimes occur in Maine Coons.

Other experts believe the Maine Coon Cat is the result of uncontrolled matings between the shorthaired cats brought to America in the seventeenth century and Angoras or Persians imported by sailors in the 1800s.

As the oldest longhaired American cat, it was fitting that the Maine Coon was voted Best Cat at North America's first professional cat show in 1895, but the breed fell into obscurity when cat fanciers began to import Persians and Siamese. The 1950s saw a revival of interest in the Maine Coon, and it was granted championship status by the Cat Fanciers Association in 1976. Its popularity has been on the rise since then.

New England cat fanciers claim the Maine Coon is the biggest (up

These pages and overleaf: **The lovable Maine Coon Cat.**

to 30 pounds), smartest, most beautiful cat in the world, and every year since the Maine Coon Cat Club was started in 1953 a Maine State Champion Coon Cat has been chosen in Skowhagan, Maine.

The ideal Maine Coon has long, soft and silky fur, and it can be in many different colors and combinations. Only the Siamese colorings are not allowed. Its body is large, muscular, broad-chested and long, so that it has a rectangular shape. A big, rounded head with high cheekbones and tufted ears complements the handsome body. The wide-set eyes are large and oval, of varying colors (green, gold, copper), in harmony with the coat. The cat's legs are medium in

length and are in proportion to the body, ending in large, round, well-tufted paws that act as snowshoes in the frozen Maine countryside. A great plume of a tail completes the cat.

Maine Coons are amiable and lovable. They are family-oriented and get along with other pets. Originally a working cat, this great hunter is intelligent, self-assured and full of pranks. Although it can endure a harsh climate, it can also adapt to a milder one.

Maine Coon kittens are slow to mature and don't reach full size until they are four to five years old. Every kitten in the litter may be a different color and pattern.

91

MALAYAN

Malayans are Burmese of another color. Since they share the same genes, they have equally perky personalities; are star athletes; extremely affectionate, preferring to sleep on the bed with their owners; are brave; and sometimes bossy and loud-mouthed. They are also smart, curious, social, and love to travel. This is definitely a cat with character.

In the United States only the sable-colored cats are recognized by the CFA as true Burmese, while cats of three other colors (champagne: a warm beige; blue: a medium blue with fawn undertones; and platinum: a light silver with fawn undertones) are classified as Malayan. In Great Britain and other parts of the world, all cats of Burmese ancestry and configuration are called Burmese, and many other colors are recognized, such as red, cream and tortoiseshell.

The show standards for Malayans, as for American Burmese, differ from those in Great Britain, Europe, Australia and New Zealand, the Americans preferring more rounded heads and eyes, whereas cat fanciers in the other countries consider moderately wedge-shaped heads and more oval eyes ideal. Malayans and Burmese in all countries have golden eyes.

Although Malayans are registered separately, they can be born spontaneously of Burmese parents. This is because they are descendants of *Wong Mau*, a hybrid, and the several Siamese used in the early Burmese breeding programs — all contributing different color genes. *(See Burmese)*

These pages: **The Malayan Cat.**

Left, above and below: The Malayan has all the personality and curiosity of its Burmese and Siamese cousins.

MANX

Manx kittens have been divided into four groups, depending on how little or how much tail they possess. The true exhibition Manx, known as a 'rumpy,' has no tail at all, and may have a dimple in its place. 'Rumpy-risers' have a few tail vertebrae, which form a little knob. 'Stumpies' have a short tail, often curved or kinked, which is usually movable. And 'longies' have an almost normal tail, though upon close scrutiny one can see it is somewhat shorter. All of the above may be registered as Manx cats, but only the rumpies may be exhibited. Rumpy-risers without any visible stump are allowed in a few associations, but the judges always are partial to the rumpies.

However, the last three categories are appreciated for their Manx genes and are not shunned in breeding programs, so they don't miss all the fun. In fact, they're very much in demand, because a continuous cross of two tailless Manx cats can result in malformations of the vertebrae, or an anomaly of the structure of the anus, causing some kittens to die before birth or soon after.

The Manx is produced by the effect of one dominant gene only, and one-fourth of the kittens conceived from Manx-to-Manx matings do not survive to birth because they have inherited two dominant Manx tailless genes. Those which do survive have one gene for taillessness and one gene for a normal tail. But breeders prefer to cross Manx with Manx, rather than with British or American Shorthairs, in order to be more certain of obtaining the desired totally rounded look and double coat of fur, and also to develop the breed strongly, it is absolutely necessary to cross the tailless cats with those Manx which have some tail.

According to the British standard, a Manx should have a rump 'as round as an orange,' and the CFA states: 'The overall impression of the Manx cat is that of roundness.' Therefore, the ideal Manx has a round head and muzzle, prominent cheeks with fat whisker pads, a slight nose dip, medium-sized ears with rounded tips, round eyes, a thick neck and a short back, which arches from the shoulders to the rounded rump, with the rump being considerably higher than the shoulders. The hind legs are longer than the front legs and are thick and sturdy. The body is like a barrel and covered with a plush double coat, consisting of a dense, cottony undercoat and a glossy, longer overcoat, like that of a rabbit. All colors are permitted, and thus there are solid-color, bi-color, tabby, calico, marbled, tortoiseshell and more. The Manx resembles a rabbit in more ways than one: owing to its hind legs being longer than its front legs, it has a bobbing, hare-like gait.

There are several tales which attempt to explain the origin of the Manx.

These pages: **The Manx Cat.**

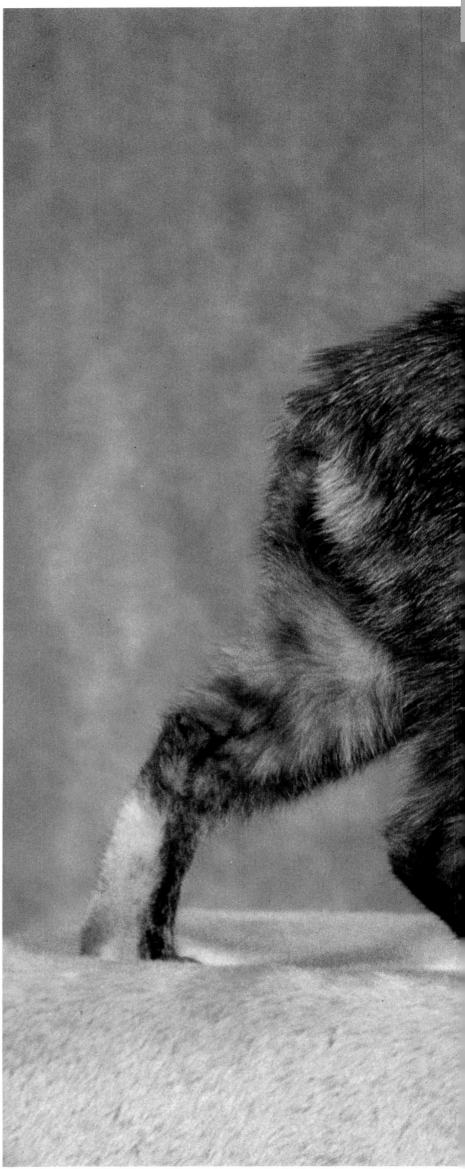

**The Manx's heavy, glossy double coat comes in a wide variety of colors,
from blue** (*facing page*) **to white** (*above*) **to calico.**

In 1588, one of the galleons of the Spanish armada, which had a tailless Tom on board, sank close to the Isle of Man, upon which the tailless Tom swam to shore and started his own breeding program. This is not entirely unbelievable because Manx have an inherent love of water.

Another story states that Phoenicians, merchants and Mediterranean sailors spread these cats from Japan, China, and Malaysia. This has since been disproved by the discovery that the Japanese Bobtail carries a recessive bobtail gene that breeds bobtails every time, whereas the Manx, as mentioned above, is produced by a dominant gene.

In another account, Father Noah gets the credit (or blame) for the cats losing their tails. As the waters started to rise, he is said to have suddenly closed the doors of his ark on the cats' tails.

An old poem suggests the cats of the Isle of Man may have lost their tails 'by sedentary habits, as do the rabbits.'

A more recent legend tells of Irish invaders who stole the cats' tails for helmet plumes, so that mother cats gently bit the tails from

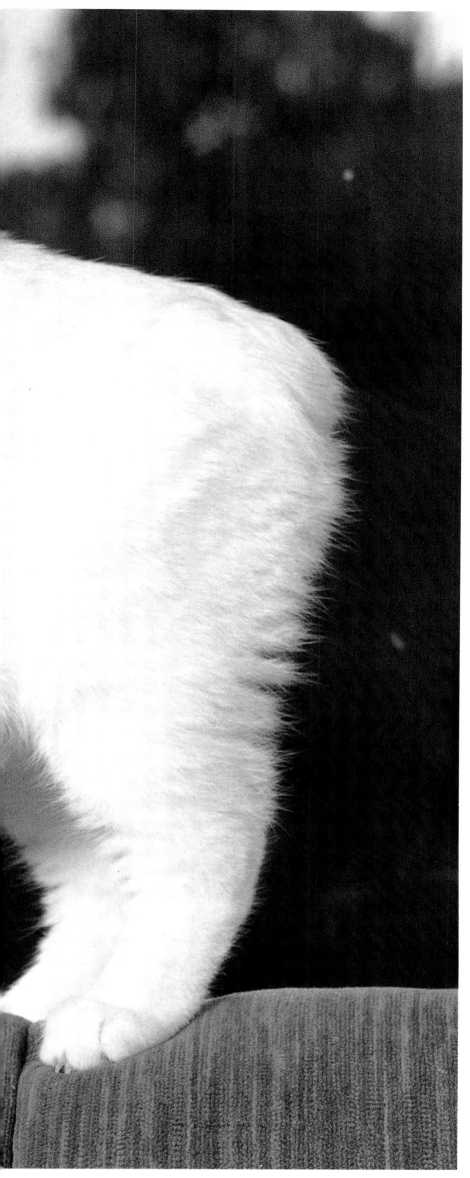

Left: **From its head to its tailless rump, the Manx gives the impression of roundness. Note the long hind legs on the cat *above*.**

their kittens to alleviate the pain of the future mutilation of their offspring.

Whatever its origin, the original mutation must have occurred long ago, for the Manx breed was well established and popular before the turn of the century. A cat fancier wrote in 1900: 'The Manx is considered by many people as a natural curiosity. It differs from the ordinary cat but little, except in the absence of a tail or even an apology for one. The hind legs are thicker and rather longer than the ordinary cat's and it runs more like a hare.' The writer continued: 'The Manx cat came from the Isle of Man originally and is a distinct breed.' In 1901 a Manx Club was formed in Britain, and King Edward VII is reputed to have owned several pet Manx cats.

The tailless cat arrived early in North America, too, for it shows up in pedigree cat registers. While the Manx lost some popularity in Britain in the 1930s and suffered, as all cats did, during the war years, it became more popular again after the war on both sides of the Atlantic.

Throughout history the breed has had a band of followers fanatically devoted to its interests. Owners of Manx cats praise their intelligence, buoyant spirit, friendliness with everyone, even though they may become especially attached to one person, and excellent hunting ability.

The inhabitants of the Isle of Man are so proud of their national feline that they have minted a coin with its image.

Above: **A beautiful tabby Manx. The Manx has a reputation for getting along well with dogs.**

Above: **A pair of Manx kittens, a Bicolor and a Blue. Note the absence of a tail on the Blue.**

YOUR CAT'S HEALTH

Cats are basically healthy animals so, with a few precautions, the cat owner should enjoy his pet for many years. Perhaps the most important factor in a cat's health is its first visit to the veterinarian. It will receive its shots and a thorough examination. The veterinarian will check for parasites and advise the owner concerning the proper diet for the cat.

The veterinarian is a trained professional who should be considered a partner in the care of the pet. With regular visits for check-ups and booster shots, the cat will be accustomed to the vet's office. In the event of an emergency, this familiarity will assist both the veterinarian and owner in avoiding further trauma to the cat.

Although cats are hardy pets, if the cat develops any of the following symptoms, it should be taken to the veterinarian or the local pet emergency clinic immediately:

1. Unusual lethargy, which may be accompanied by straining at the litter box. The abdomen may feel full and/or hard. This may indicate a blockage in the urinary tract and is fatal if not treated. The next day may be too late! This problem occurs quite often in neutered male cats which are fed dry cat foods that are high in ash.
2. Severe, prolonged diarrhea, which may be a symptom of internal parasites, feline distemper or protozoans.
3. Red, watery eyes may indicate feline rhinotracheitis or a cold.
4. Nasal discharge may also indicate feline rhinotracheitis, a cold or an allergy.
5. Swelling or lumps in or on the cat's body which increase gradually may be cancer or abscesses.

Bright, clear eyes *(above)* **and a glistening coat** *(facing page)* **are signs of a healthy cat.** *Below:* **Veterinary technicians in a classroom.**

6. Nasal discharge, repeated coughing and sneezing are symptoms of allergy, pneumonitis or feline rhinotracheitis.
7. Repeated vomiting is an indication of either infection by a virus or internal parasites, both of which can be fatal if neglected.
8. A dull, patchy coat which sheds severely can be a symptom of many problems which a veterinarian is best qualified to investigate.

In fact, all the above symptoms are just that — symptoms — and a visit to the veterinarian is the only way to find out exactly what is wrong with the cat.

There are a number of viruses that infect the cat, including rabies, feline distemper, coryza, leptospirosis, pneumonia and feline rhinotracheitis. Parasites that affect the cat include hookworms, roundworms, tapeworms, lice, fleas, ticks and earmites. Other problems involve fungi (like ringworm) or microscopic parasites (like protozoans), which cause coccidiosis or feline infectious anemia. Very few of the feline diseases can be transmitted to the cat owner. The only precautions that need to be taken are normal sanitary measures and caution in changing the litter box. That particular chore should be avoided if the cat owner is pregnant, since some feline diseases and parasites can affect the unborn child.

This section is meant only to guide the cat owner. The veterinarian should be the final word on all aspects of the cat's health and the doctor's instructions should be followed to the letter in all instances.

A healthy cat will be a pleasant companion for many years, enriching the lives of the family around it.

Christmas can be harmful to your cat. Poinsettias *(left)* **are poisonous, while garland and electric lights** *(above)* **can be fatal if swallowed.** *Below:* **An Abyssinian and friend.**

NORWEGIAN FOREST CAT

The Norwegian Forest Cat loves the outdoors, and it is especially well-equipped, mentally and physically, to survive harsh northern winters. It has the intelligence, independence, courage, caution, and speed needed to be a fine hunter. Its unique heavy, thick double coat affords great protection against the cold. The shorter, woolly undercoat keeps the body warm, while the longer, oily, outer coat resists rain and snow. If caught in a heavy rain, it takes about 15 minutes for the coat to dry. This hardy Scandinavian cat has a robust, muscular body with powerful legs. Its remarkable claws enable it to climb rocks as well as trees.

The 'Norsk Skaukatt,' as it is called in Norway, has a round and strong head, with large, attentive eyes, tall, tufted ears, high cheek bones, slightly up-tilted nose, and firm chin. It has a rich, fluffy ruff with a full frontal bib and abundant fur on the sides and back of the neck. The body is moderately long and the hind legs are longer than the front legs. Its broad chest and considerable girth give the cat a powerful appearance. It carries its long, thickly-furred tail high. In summer, after shedding, only the ear and toe tufts and tail reveal that the Norwegian Forest Cat is a longhair.

This breed is believed to have evolved because of the extreme conditions in the Norwegian woodlands. It is probable the cat's ancestors were shorthaired cats from southern Europe and longhaired cats from Asia Minor, brought to Scandinavia by traders and travelers centuries ago. Records of the Norwegian Forest Cat go back to antiquity. It is mentioned in Old Norse mythology and is referred to as a 'fairy cat' in fables written between 1837 and 1852. Because this feline definitely predates the Persian in Norway, it is not basically a Persian hybrid. However, once the Persians landed in the North, cat nature being what it is, the two breeds occasionally got together, so there certainly exist some Norwegian Forest Cats with Persian blood in them.

A group of breeders began to develop the Norwegian Forest Cat breed in earnest in the 1930s, and at least one cat was exhibited at a show in Oslo before the Second World War. After the war, in the early 1970s, there was a resurgence of interest in this handsome cat, which comes in all colors except Siamese pattern, and the people of Norway decided to preserve the breed as a living monument to Norwegian culture. The Fédération Internationale Féline d'Europe recognized the Norwegian Forest Cat in 1977, and it is now accepted for competition at all European cat shows, but it is not yet recognized or bred in the United States.

This good natured, innovative cat, with wits sharpened in the wild, is inventive about opening doors and latches, so, if it becomes bored indoors, the cat may simply open the door and go outside and roam free for awhile. It will most likely return and let itself in again, because this cat is affectionate and devoted to its owner.

OCICAT

The Ocicat is an ideal pet for those who love dramatically beautiful animals with a friendly personality. *Tonga*, the first kitten, reminded its breeder of a baby ocelot, and hence the name 'Ocicat.' Combining a wild appearance with a gentle disposition, it has also been compared with the ancient Egyptian fishing cats and the Egyptian Mau, as well as the man-made Spotted Tabby Oriental.

The Ocicat is a hybrid, initially achieved by crossing a chocolate-point Siamese stud with an Abyssinian pointed Siamese queen. Their spotted, tabby patterned offspring were used to perpetuate the genetic inheritance, and thus was created the Ocicat. Since then, American Shorthairs have also been introduced into the breeding program, and breeders are working assiduously with the three breeds — Siamese, Abyssinian, and American Shorthair — to improve this splendid cat which looks as if it just walked out of the jungle.

Females are medium size, while males are very large, 12 to 15 pounds. This is a well muscled cat, with long legs. The head is well-proportioned, with large ears and eyes and a fine muzzle.

There are eight different color combinations of the polka-dotted, short and shiny coat: silver with black dots; blue with slate-blue dots; tawny (buff or ruddy) with black or brown dots; dusky golden (bronze) with tarnished gold dots; golden with cinnamon dots (unique to Ocicats); chocolate with dull chocolate dots; sienna with beige or ecru dots; and lavender with lavender dots. Eyes are copper, green, yellow, hazel, or blue green, and have dark lids, with a rim of the lightest color of the coat around them. The tail is long and tapering.

The Ocicat was accepted for registration by the Cat Fanciers Association in the 1960s.

The Norwegian Forest Cat may be descended from the European Wild Cat *(at top)*. The spotted Ocicat *(right)* bears a striking resemblance to the wild cat *below*.

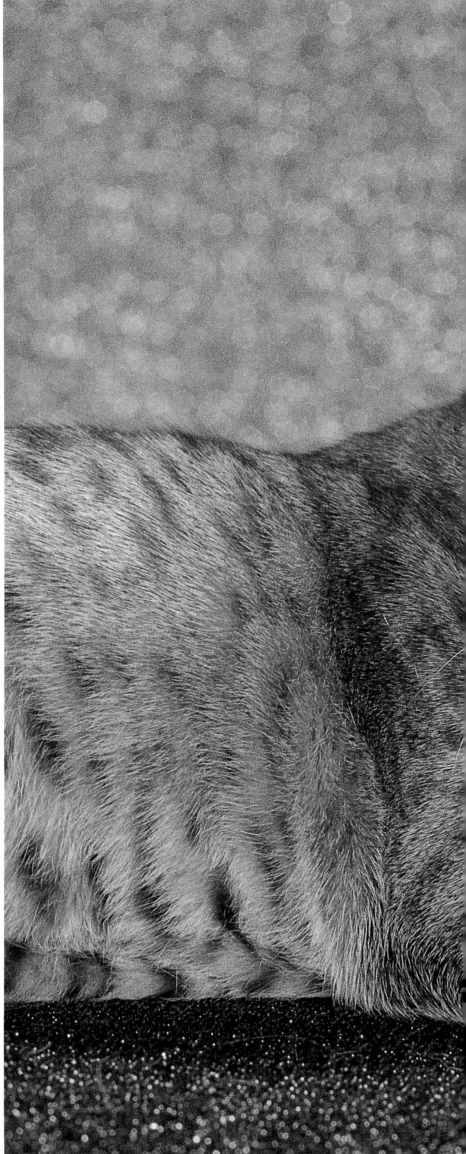

These pages: **The Ocicat.**

ORIENTAL SHORTHAIR

The Oriental Shorthair is a solid-colored Siamese cat which was created by breeders. In 1950, some British cat lovers took the Siamese standard and added new colors to the traditional body type, called 'foreign,' by arranged matings between Siamese for type and other shorthair cats for color. Each color is known as an individual breed in England and Europe, so they are referred to as Foreign White, Foreign Lilac, etc, and collectively as Foreign Shorthairs, whereas all are called Oriental Shorthairs and judged as one breed in the United States. These solid-colored felines would have come to prominence sooner were it not for chance and choice. The first cats arriving from Siam (now Thailand) in the late nineteenth century, which attracted the attention of Western cat fanciers, were colorpointed. In this group there were some solid-colored cats, and some were exhibited, but by the 1920s the Siamese Cat Club in Britain decided to promote only the blue-eyed, pointed Siamese.

From the time of this official shunning, solid-colored, foreign-type cats declined in popularity with Western cat lovers. There is mention, however, by a German professor, writing just before the Second World War, of 'beautiful strains with good capability of inheritance,' and describing all-black and all-blue cats of foreign configuration.

During the war, owing to restrictions and the state of the economy, breeding probably came to a halt, but after the war, in Britain, a breeding program was undertaken for the production of all-brown coated cats with a foreign body type. Thus was born the Brown Oriental, which is identical with the Havana in Britain *(see Havana Brown)*. This new brown breed was the advance scout for the Siamese-shaped white cats soon to step into the limelight.

In 1962 three British breeders and geneticists launched separate programs to develop a breed of true-breeding, blue-eyed white cats, and in 1964 they got together. By the following year, the manager of a cat show held at York remarked: 'The BBC television paid us a visit and viewers were able to see us all in action. There was special interest in Miss Turner's experimental "white Siamese".'

Created by crossing white Domestic Shorthairs to Siamese, the White Oriental looks like fine porcelain, with its gleaming white fur and brilliant blue eyes and, unlike other blue-eyed white cats, this striking cat is never deaf. While green- or golden-eyed white Orientals are allowed in the United States, blue-eyed cats are

continued on page 120

Below: **An Oriental Shorthair and its cousin, the Siamese.** *Facing page:*
A Foreign Lilac, aka Lavender Oriental Shorthair.

Below: **A Blue Oriental Shorthair.**

Notice the similarities between the Oriental Shorthair *(right)* **and the Siamese** *(above left)* **and the Colorpoint Shorthair** *(above right).*

continued from page 116
preferred. Full recognition with championship status was granted in 1977, and the breed had its first grand champion in 1979.

Because lilac point Siamese were repeatedly used as mates in the Chestnut Brown breeding program, a great many Siamese-type solid lilacs were born and the Foreign Lilac breed achieved full recognition simultaneously with the Foreign White breed.

While the Foreign Whites and Foreign Lilacs were being created, some other cat fanciers decided to develop tabby cats with Siamese shape, and several were shown and won prizes. Another British breeder became intrigued with the spotted cats in Egyptian frescoes, and began producing spotted cats with Siamese form, apart from the Egyptian Mau breeding program in the United States. She started with a Siamese-type tabby (produced during the development of the tabby point Siamese). She then added two Chestnut Browns with tabby points; the progeny were beautifully marked spotted tabbies with foreign bodies.

An accidental mating between a chinchilla Persian and a chocolate point Siamese in 1970, resulting in the birth of two Siamese-type shaded silver kittens, started Oriental breeding in a new direction in Britain. It was discovered that the inhibitor gene responsible for silver, shaded and smoke colorings is dominant and independent of the Siamese gene, and breeders in Britain are now busy creating tipped silver and smoke varieties.

Certain American cat fanciers pioneered North American Oriental Shorthairs by establishing an international breed club, which many Siamese breeders joined. They chose the name 'Oriental Shorthair' and the Cat Fanciers Association granted provisional recognition in 1976. The breed reached championship status only a year later, and within one season this svelte Siamese cousin won more top awards and grand championships than any other breed new to championship. It was also featured among the CFA's all-American top twenty cats.

Oriental Shorthairs are now well-established worldwide, and the breed has reached new heights in America, with 26 different colors, divided into five groups: solids, shadeds, smokes, tabbies, and particolors. Still in the experimental stage are even more colors, such as Caramel Oriental, Apricot Oriental, and Beige Oriental, all with pale green eyes.

The Oriental Shorthair show requirements are the same as those for the Siamese, with the exception of the blue eyes. In Britain, as mentioned, Foreign Whites must have blue eyes; medium size; long, lissome, tubular and leggy; fine-boned; long, tapering, wedge-shaped head with a fine muzzle; large, flared and pointed ears; almond-shaped eyes; long, tapering tail; short, fine, tight, and glossy coat.

In personality, the Oriental Shorthair also resembles its cousin, the Siamese (after all, only one or two color genes separate the two breeds), in that both demand a lot of attention, and, in turn, give total devotion, and are talkative, agile, intelligent, independent and inquisitive companions.

Raising Oriental Shorthairs is not necessarily for those who love tranquility, for the lively kittens especially enjoy practicing their climbing skills on the furniture and the curtains.

In Great Britain, this svelte Oriental Shorthair *(above)* would be judged
as a Foreign Black.

PERSIAN

Although the Persian cat, with its glorious fur, pampered look, and aristocratic bearing, epitomizes the pedigreed cat and all that goes with expensive tastes and a life of luxury, its origin is obscure.

Longhaired cats were first introduced to Europe in the sixteenth century; many early records referred to them as Angoras, while early British books named them French cats, probably because they arrived in France first and came to Britain from there. *(See Turkish Angora)*

Later, in the eighteenth century, the first Persian cat was taken to Italy by the explorer Pietro della Valle. A century later the Persian breed was introduced to France and England, where, through crossbreeding with the Angora, it gained a silkier coat and a greater variety of colors.

It is thought that both the Angora and the Persian may have originated in Russia, even though they came to Europe from Turkey and Persia (Iran), because longhaired cats are more common there than in either of the other two countries. The harsh climate in Russia may have caused the evolution of the long coat. Some Asian wild cat, which came in from the cold, is doubtless the paterfamilias of the longhaired, domestic cats of today.

Cats in Persia had broader, rounder heads, smaller ears, sturdier bodies, and plusher fur than those in Turkey, which had long, pointed heads, large ears, lissome bodies and silky fur without an undercoat.

The result of the crossbreeding of the two breeds in the nineteenth century was that the Persian type was dominant and the Angora was lost in the Western World until the breed was revived in the 1950s.

continued on page 129

Below and facing page: **Whether for show or just companionship, these Persian kittens will make delightful pets.**

Above: A gorgeous Shaded Silver Persian in typical Persian repose. The white undercoat on the back, flanks, head and tail of a Shaded Silver is tipped in black. The legs should be the same tone as the face. Shaded Silver kittens are born dark, often with tabby markings.

continued from page 124
Adding to the Angora's demise was the fact that people admired Persians more, and the royal stamp of approval was given by Queen Victoria, who owned two blues, and the Prince of Wales (who became King Edward VII), who donated and presented a special prize for Persians at a cat show.

Persians arrived in North America from Europe at the end of the nineteenth century and were soon more popular than the native Maine Coons. Americans set to work at once developing a breed type, based on the standards set up by the British, with an even more chunky build and more profuse coat. The British today prefer the older, less stocky shape.

World War I intervened, causing a slowdown in cat breeding in Europe, but once it was over Persians flourished again. Then came World War II, which nearly put a total stop to cat breeding in Britain, at which point the Americans gained the first place in Persian breeding.

At the first official cat show in Britain, which was held in 1871, mostly black, blue and white Persians were exhibited, but other colors were gradually added. Now there are at least 30 color varieties of Persian, albeit not all are accepted for competition in all countries. In Great Britain each color variety is considered a separate breed, and they are called 'Longhairs' rather than Persians. In the United States all of the colors are listed as varieties of Persians. Some organizations call colorpointed cats Himalayans, and solid chocolate or solid lilac cats Kashmirs. The English consider all of them to be Longhairs.

The CFA has divided Persian colors into several divisions for show purposes: (1) solid colors, including solid chocolate and lilac; (2) shaded (tipped) colors; (3) smokes, tabby patterns; (4) parti-colored; and (5) point-restricted colors.

White Persians were regarded as status symbols in London at the turn of the century. The earliest cats had blue eyes, long, pointed faces, and were frequently deaf. Today there are three types: blue-eyed whites; orange-eyed whites; and odd-eyed whites. Some white kittens are born with small clusters of colored hair on their heads, revealing the underlying color genotype, and many cat

Facing page: **A Peke-Face Red Persian. Note the snub-nose similar to that of a Pekinese dog.** *Above:* **A champion Persian and the next generation — a fluffy Persian kitten** *(below).*

Left: **The Smoke Tortoiseshell, a variety found only in the United States.** *Above:* **A striking Tabby with full coat and copper eyes.**

fanciers believe that a head smudge (which disappears at about nine months) is a sign of perfect hearing, but this is not always true.

Early black Persians, like more like white Persians, were more like Angoras, but these features have now been bred out and current black Persians have round heads and cobby bodies. A jet black is required, with no tinge of rustiness, white hairs or tabby markings. Black Persians with orange eyes are striking cats.

Blue Persians have always been the most popular solid-colored Persians, perhaps stemming from Queen Victoria's early choice of a pair of blues. Lighter shades of blue are preferred and, combined with copper-colored eyes, make a very beautiful cat.

Tortoiseshell (or Calico) Persians are comparatively rare because of the difficulty in breeding them, nearly all tortoiseshells being females and the few males being sterile. This was, and is, an invitation for deception. People have been persuaded to pay large sums to acquire a stud tortoiseshell.

In an 1849 issue of a popular magazine, *Ladies' Cabinet*, there was a story about a tortoiseshell Tom auctioned for 22.50, a very high price then, to an elderly lady. She took the cat home and it seemed to settle in, but in a few days the cat was looking sickly. The lady did everything she could think of to restore her valuable purchase back to health, even going so far as to give the cat a hot milk bath, because of the common belief that cats dislike water. She convinced the cat to sit in the warm milk and to her consternation the milk started turning the orange color of the cat. When she lifted the Tom out of the basin, it was no longer a tortoiseshell, but a black-and-white Longhair.

Tabbies were included in the classification for the 1871 cat show, with silver tabbies being the most popular. Shaded and tipped Persian varieties developed out of the early silver tabbies, the best-known member of the group being the silver chinchilla. A famous early chinchilla was named *Silver Lambkin*, and it is believed he sired both silver and golden kittens. The characteristic feature is an undercoat of one color with guard hairs tipped to varying extent with a contrasting color. Chinchillas have a more delicate appearance than other Persians, but they, too, are sturdy cats.

Recognized for competition as a separate variety in the United States and Canada are Peke-faced Persians, bred only in red and red tabby versions. They have the same body characteristics as Persians, but 'the head should resemble as much as possible that of the

continued on page 134

Below: A Bicolor Persian.

continued from page 131
Pekinese dog from which it gets its name. There should be a decidedly wrinkled muzzle.' Some of these cats have breathing difficulties and runny eyes owing to blockages or distortions of the ducts that cause tears to drain into the nose.

Some more recent popular Persian varieties include dilute calicos, which have patched coats of blue and cream with white; smoke Persians with white undercoat and contrasting tipped overcoats; and lilac-cream, which have shades of lilac and cream softly intermingled throughout the coat.

Adopting a Persian means taking on the responsibility of daily grooming of this cat's magnificent, full coat with a steel comb, for a little knot in the fur will soon become a large tangle if left unattended and will cause pain as it pulls against the cat's tender skin. Persians should be powdered lightly with French chalk or baby powder to keep the hair separated. In addition, regular bathing is required to remove excess oil from the coat.

A Persian may repay all this care by nudging with its head, giving gentle 'love bites' and purring purrs like thunder or, upon being picked up, by wrapping its front legs around its owner's neck.

This is a calm-appearing cat with a strong temperament and a great desire for affection. It adapts well to apartment living and can happily be the only pet. Because of its bulky body and short, sturdy legs, a Persian is less active than other breeds, although most are playful and some are good mousers.

RAGDOLL

This is a plush cat come to life, for, when picked up, it relaxes completely and flops over like a ragdoll. When a cat of this breed is lying on your bed, you might mistake it for a toy cat.

And it has a personality to match — placid, fearless, and noncombative. This puts the Ragdoll at risk from other animals and children and it should, therefore, not be allowed out alone, as it might lose some fur — or worse.

A legend of the Ragdoll's bendable body, intrepid attitude, and Quaker stance is that the founding matriarch of this breed, a white Persian queen, had been injured in a road accident before giving birth to her offspring, which resulted in their having an inability to feel pain or fear, or fight other animals, as well as having a hang-loose body to match.

Geneticists don't agree with this explanation, and state that the feline's flexible body, mild temperament, and refusal to fight come from the gene mix.

They say the above mentioned characteristics are the result of too frequent selective breeding among domestic cats. In the beginning, the Ragdoll was a hybrid breed resulting from the mating of a white Persian and a seal point Birman, and the later mating of the kittens from that coupling with a sable Burmese.

There is controversy over how many different breed characteristics should be combined in the development of an acceptable breed, and Ragdolls are not recognized by the CFA; however, they have gained acceptance in several other associations, the breed having first been recognized for competition in 1965.

Exceptionally large and heavy, Ragdolls are similar to Birmans. They have big, oval, blue eyes, and medium-sized ears set high on a modified wedge-shaped head. They are broad at the chest and hindquarters, with heavy-boned, medium-length legs ending in large, round, tufted paws.

The medium to long coat comes in seal point, chocolate point, blue point, and lilac point, with varying amounts of white about the face, neck, chest, under the body and under the tail, in addition to the four white paws.

With only a few Ragdolls in existence and all of those in California, much work will be necessary before cat fanciers consider the breed as established. Yet they seem to be on their way, for today Ragdolls are mated only to Ragdolls, and breed true.

Right: **This Shaded Silver Persian kitten is certain to grow into a beauty.**

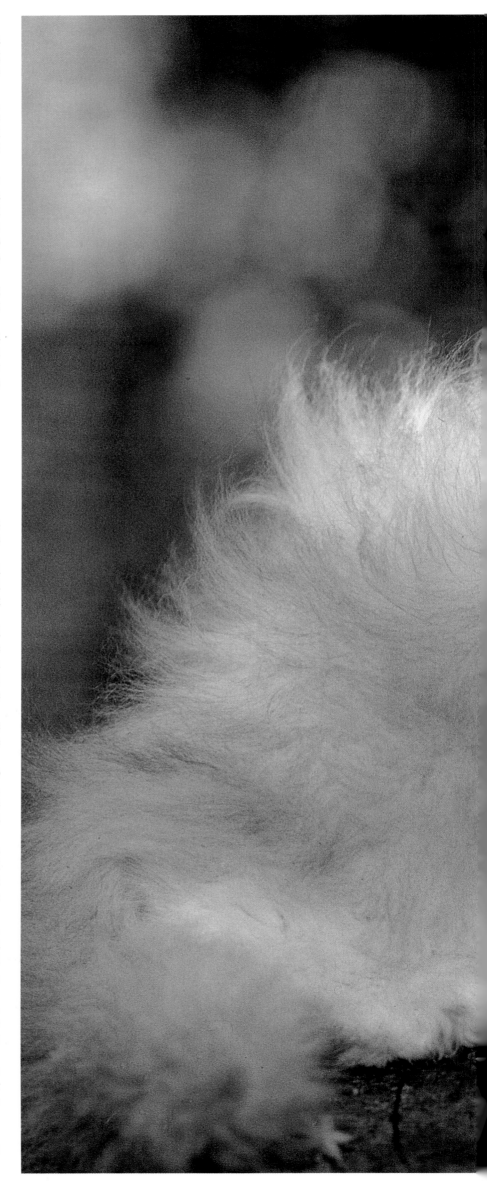

REX

The curly-coated Cornish and Devon Rex cats, with their big eyes and ears and long, whip-like tails, are for avant-garde tastes, and are also ideal for those who love cats but are allergic to them. Because Rex cats have a finer coat than other shorthairs and rarely shed hair, people who normally have trouble breathing around other cats can tolerate these unique felines.

The first known Rex cat was born in East Germany in 1946, but breeders did not start a breeding program with this cat until 1951, a year after the Cornish Rex appeared on the scene. This second spontaneous mutation, which is the same as the Cornish Rex, was discovered by Dr Scheur-Karpin. It is known as the 'Lammchen' line, after its name. *Kallibunker*, the first Cornish Rex, was born in

1950 of a domestic shorthair mother and an unknown father, on a farm in Bodmin Moor, Cornwall, England. His owner, Mrs Nina Ennismore, got in touch with an expert cat breeder and rabbit fancier, and by breeding *Kallibunker* back to his mother, more Rex kittens were produced. The recessive mutation was named after the similar mutation found in the rabbits.

Two of *Kallibunker*'s descendants were imported to America in 1957 and founded the Cornish Rex line there.

Then, in 1960, a curly-coated feral cat was observed living in the vicinity of a used-up tin mine near Buckfastleigh, Devon. A young tortie and white stray, adopted by a neighboring resident, mated with this wild cat and gave birth to a kitten with curly fur, which was also adopted and called *Kirlee*.

Kirlee's owner contacted *Kallibunker*'s owner and the two cats were bred. To the breeders' surprise, only straight-haired kittens resulted from several matings. It was then realized that the two lines

These pages: **The Rex Cat.**

The curly-coated Rex — a Tabby (left) **and a Blue** (above).

represented unrelated mutations and would have to be advanced by separate breeding programs. They also decided to breed toward two distinct body types.

Three German Rexes were sent to the United States in the early 1960s, and when crossed with Cornish cats, curly kittens were created. The two distinct breeds — Cornish and Devon Rexes — were recognized for championship competition in 1967 in Britain. In America, the Cat Fanciers Association established the Cornish Rex as distinct from the Devon Rex in 1979.

Cornish Rexes have essentially foreign (Siamese) bodies with an arched back, long, straight legs, and a foreign-type head with a long Roman nose. They have curly whiskers.

With huge ears, large, usually golden, eyes, and a short nose, set in a dainty, triangular head, Devon Rexes look like impish pixies. Their heads are based on *Kirlee*'s. The whisker pads of these charmers are more prominent than those of Cornish Rexes and the whiskers may be curly, stubs, or absent. They have fine, silky coats, which feel like suede or brushed corduroy, with only a few guard hairs. Their bodies are similar to those of Cornish Rexes, but with a broader chest and a straight back.

Both Rexes are accepted in nearly all colors appropriate to American and British Shorthairs. The Si-Rex is an unofficial name for Rex cats with Siamese colorpoints. The best way to groom Rex cats is with firm strokes of the hand, and they purr with pleasure during the whole process.

Owing to their finer fur Rex cats must be protected from extreme heat and cold and should not be allowed out in very hot or very cold weather. Their normal body temperature is one degree higher than in other breeds and they always feel warm to the touch. This higher metabolism results in huge appetites, but the food is rapidly burned off. A high-fat diet to supplement the higher metabolism is suggested, but Rexes should not be allowed to overeat or they will become fat.

The Rex could be called a lap cat, but it can also run very fast. It is extremely inquisitive, as well as affectionate, independent, very intelligent and generally talkative, in a somewhat high-pitched voice.

Cornish and Devon kittens are tiny and look like little mice at birth. Some may be hairless. They are normally active at a very early age and exhibit the persistent inquisitiveness which is typical of both strains.

Above: **A pair of Rex cats.**

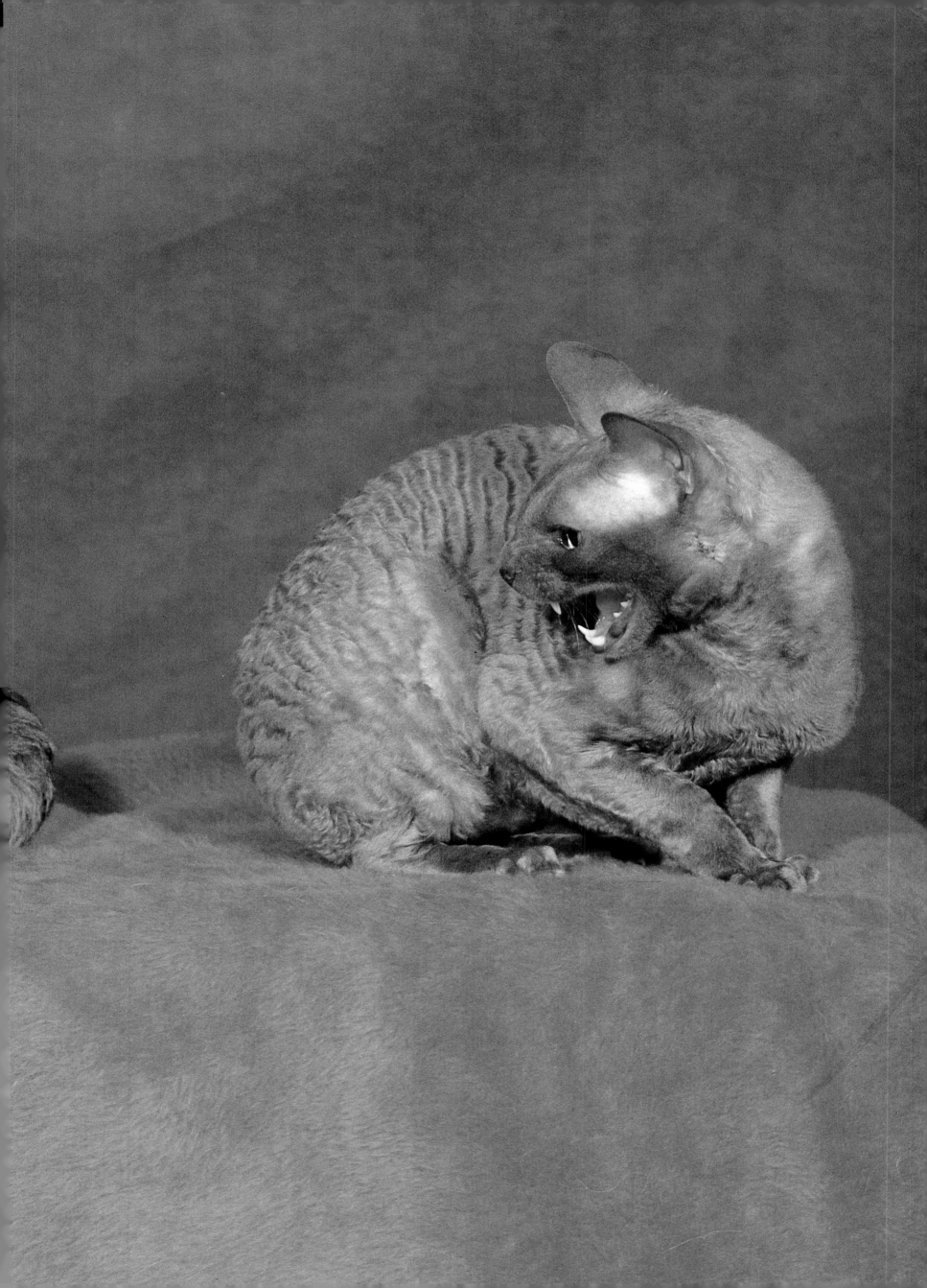

RUSSIAN BLUE

The most distinctive feature of the Russian Blue is its short, dense, plush, upstanding double coat, like that of a seal or a beaver, which feels silky and soft. This graceful cat is a bright, even blue, with the silver-tipped guard hairs giving the coat a silvery sheen. It has vivid green eyes and mauve or lavender-pink noseleather and paw pads.

The Russian Blue is a medium-to-large Oriental-type, and is leggy, with a long, slender neck and tail, and a lithe, graceful body. Its head is wedge-shaped, shorter than a Siamese's, with prominent whisker pads, large ears, more pointed than rounded, and a strong chin. The eyes are almond-shaped and slant toward the nose. This cat has a serene expression on its face and appears to be smiling.

Another unique characteristic of the Russian Blue is its soft-spoken, almost inaudible voice. The breed is so quiet that you may not know when a queen is in season.

Russian Blues are very affectionate with each other and make excellent parents. There are usually one or two litters of four to five kittens each year, cared for by both parents. They are born with fluffy coats that may have faint tabby markings until the adult coat develops.

Also demonstrably affectionate toward their owners, Russian Blues can be reserved with strangers. This tranquil, somewhat shy cat likes calm surroundings and thus fits in best with a family without unruly children or undue noise.

While Russian Blues love to be indoors and sit by the fire, they are physically hardy and robust, and, if necessary, can stand the cold as did their Russian ancestors.

British sailors visiting the White Sea port of Archangel are believed to have brought the first Russian Blues to Western Europe in the 1860s, and before 1900 they were most often known as 'Archangel Blues.' There seemed to be some confusion as to what was or wasn't a Russian Blue, for they were also called 'Maltese Blues,' 'Spanish Blues,' 'Chartreuse Blues,' 'British Blues' and even 'American Blues.' This may have been because they were outcrossed to British Blues and Blue-point Siamese, since there were few cats of the same breed to mate with. For a time, too, the Russian Blue closely resembled the Siamese, which resemblance has since been bred out. This quiet cat finally acquired its current name in the 1940s, evidence definitely suggesting that the breed originated in Russia, because similar cats exist there, especially in the colder regions.

Pages 142 – 147: **The Russian Blue Cat.**

It was shown at cat shows in Great Britain around the turn of the century when all shorthaired blue cats competed in one class, whatever their body type. The British taste inclining toward cobbier, rounder cats, the lankier, longer cats seldom won many prizes, and so interest in the Russian Blue waned. In 1912 separate classes were established for British Blues and Russian Blues, and both flourished from then until World War II, when all cats suffered.

After the war, Scandinavian as well as British breeders began developing the breed, crossing Russian Blues with Siamese. This outcrossing process was carried to such lengths that the Russian Blue standard was rewritten to reflect the much more extreme foreign body type (not to mention the new voice).

At last, in 1965, a group of British breeders began a concerted effort to return the breed to its original confirmation: a shorter, wedge-shaped head, with wide face, prominent whisker pads, and large, upright ears. The following year, the show standard was changed again, closely defining the Russian Blue as it appeared back in the 1860s and with the admonition that the 'Siamese type is undesirable.'

Russian Blue cats are a challenge to breed to the standard, because if the coat is right then the head is wrong or the ears are too small, or there is some other fault, such as white hairs in the coat. What's more, if a Russian Blue lives permanently in a warmer climate, it gradually loses its dense, shiny, seal-like coat, which becomes lighter in texture, for it is no longer needed.

Despite these difficulties, Russian Blues are popular in some parts of the world today. In Australia and New Zealand a very good strain has been bred from expatriate British cats, and Black and White Russians are also recognized there. Though fewer in number than in the past, there are still enthusiastic supporters of the breed in Britain, America and Scandinavia.

An explanation of their decline in popularity may be that, because Russian Blues have small litters and are difficult to produce to standard, they are not a good business proposition for anyone looking for fast profits. Another explanation is that there are now many more blue cats from which to choose than there were when the Russian Blues first appeared in the West, and so cat fanciers are sharing their affections with more breeds.

SCOTTISH FOLD

The Scottish Fold, with its small, folded ears, large round eyes and rather wistful expression, looks like a plush toy or a ceramic figurine.

A cat of this unique type, brought from China to England toward the end of the 1880s, caused no small stir, since up to that time all the cats of the world had upright ears. It is not known whether this Chinese cat had any direct descendants.

The current breed originated in Perthshire, Scotland, when, one day in 1961, a shepherd noticed that one of the kittens born on the farm had folded ears. The shepherd, William Ross, realizing the rarity of the occurrence, kept watch over *Susie*, the feline with the floppy ears, and when, two years later, she brought forth two droopy-eared kittens, he adopted one, a white female, which he named *Snooks*, and registered her.

From then on, a breeding program was begun and, while investigating the genetics of this natural mutation, it was discovered that folded ears come from a single, dominant gene. The breeders also became aware that some Folds have thicker, shorter tails with a rounded tip. At first, they were in favor of this feature as contributing to the overall rounded look of the cat, but, when they found that some of these cats have thickened limbs as well, the breeders changed their minds and it is now considered an unwelcome abnormality.

These pages: **The Scottish Fold Cat.**

Facing page, left and above: **These Scottish Fold kittens display the typical feline curiosity and agility that lead to unusual perches.**

Although the Scottish Fold was originally registered in England, the privilege was rescinded when it was discovered the single, dominant gene could have a crippling effect, namely, overgrowth of the cartilage at the joints, resulting in thickened limbs. Another concern was that the folded ears would make it difficult to keep the cats free from ear mites and that they would be prone to deafness.

Breeders refute these latter suggestions by saying that only the usual hygiene required to keep upright ears free from mites is necessary, and state that several early Folds were white, which are always prone to deafness. They have kept the incidence of thickening limbs very low by breeding Folds with normal tails to British Shorthairs or to American Shorthairs.

Thus, British breeders have had to register their cats with overseas associations, and there are now more Scottish Folds being bred in the United States than in Britain. They were first registered in the Cat Fanciers Association in 1974 and received championship status in 1976.

The Scottish Fold, which is a medium-sized breed, is a shorthaired cat and comes in 23 recognized colors and patterns. Its body is short and slightly rounded, with agile legs of intermediate length and a wide and round head on a short and strong neck. Its tail should be well-proportioned and flexible.

These sweet-natured and friendly cats are content living indoors, but enjoy an occasional hunting outing, for they are excellent mousers. They are good parents and have three or four kittens in a litter. At birth their ears are identical to those of their siblings. ie, the prick-eared and folded-eared kittens are identical, but at about four weeks the folded ears become visible.

Below: This tabby patterned Scottish Fold seems quite content nestled among its owner's potted plants.

SIAMESE

'An unnatural, nightmare kind of a cat' was one cat show visitor's opinion in 1871 upon viewing a Siamese. Although others may have shared this initial reaction, it wasn't long before the Siamese cat became very popular.

The King of Siam was responsible, to some degree, for increasing the popularity of the breed, for in the early 1880s he gave two Siamese cats as parting gifts to Mr Owen Gould, then English Consul-General in Bangkok, which he brought to London and exhibited at the Crystal Palace, where they achieved great success as crowd pleasers.

In 1890 Siamese cats arrived on American shores, probably as a gift from the King of Siam to an American friend, and were soon seen in shows here. They were greatly admired and brought prices as high as $1000 each.

By 1892, the first Siamese breed standard had been written, describing this distinctive feline as follows: 'A somewhat curious and striking cat of medium size, if weighty not showing bulk, as this would detract from the admired, svelte appearance. In type, in every particular the reverse of the ideal shorthaired domestic cat, and with properly preserved contrasts in colors, a very handsome animal, often distinguished by a kink in the tail.'

The kink eventually came to be seen as a fault, but not before the first champion in Britain had been named — a cat called *Wankee*, born in Hong Kong in 1895, complete with a kink in its tail. Some early cats also had squinty or crossed eyes, which, together with the kink have, through selective breeding, been largely bred out.

Regarding the cat's character, a turn of the century breeder observed: 'They are dog-like in their nature, and can easily be taught to turn back somersaults, and to retrieve, and in the country take long walks like a terrier.'

continued on page 157

Above: **A Siamese (left) and its Burmese cousin (right). Contrast the present day Siamese standard** *(below),* **with lean body and wedge-shaped head, to the earlier but still popular look** *(right).*

Above: A Siamese and friend.

Left: **An attentive group of Siamese.** *Above:* **This Siamese is a very inquisitive cat, happy to spend hours investigating its owner's flowerbeds.**

continued from page 154

Owing at least partially to its personality, the Siamese became the fashionable cat to own in the 1920s and, despite the derogatory comment of that early cat show visitor, this was, and is, a very beautiful cat.

Since the 1902 revision of the original standard, it has evolved into a more sleek and elegant animal than was the original version.

In the late 1920s the Siamese Cat Club decided to promote only blue-eyed, pointed Siamese. Previous to that time, writers on the breed mentioned two kinds of Siamese: those with pale bodies and points and brown cats. The former were referred to then as the 'royal Siamese' or the 'royal cat of Siam,' and were more highly regarded than the brown cats, about which there is some confusion. They may have been Siamese-Burmese hybrids, which today are called 'Tonkinese.'

The CFA, in America, now recognizes four contrasting color patterns: seal point, which is the earliest and most widespread color, where the adult is beige with seal brown mask, ears, lower legs, feet, and tail; blue point, which has the same beige-colored body, but with blue-gray mask, ears, legs, feet, and tail; chocolate point, with an ivory coat and milk-chocolate points; and lilac point, with a glacial white coat and gray-pink points, including a lavender-pink nose. All have clear blue eyes.

The Governing Council of the Cat Fancy in Britain considers Red Points, Tabby Points (in varying hues), and Tortie Points (also in several colors) as Siamese, while in the US they are called 'Colorpoints.' An exquisite, new variety is the Silver, with names such as Silver Seal Tabby Point and Silver Blue Tabby Point. A Silver Tabby Point Siamese, still relatively rare, has a paler body coat than do other Siamese and is silver between the tabby stripes.

A Siamese should be medium in size, sinuous and svelte, with long legs and tail, and have a long, wedge-shaped head, forming an

A Seal Point Siamese *(left)* **and a Lilac Point Siamese** *(above).*
Overleaf: **A trio of Chocolate Point Siamese.**

equilateral triangle from nose to tips of ears, which are large, pointed and flared. The profile is straight from forehead to nose; and the vivid blue eyes are almond-shaped and slanted toward the nose in harmony with the head. This feline has fine bones and fur. Its coat is so short and tight it is almost invisible.

Although each Siamese has its own special personality, certain characteristics predominate. These are extremely intelligent, loving, independent, talkative, and active cats. They are also unpredictable, for they are very sensitive and have mood swings from placid to prickly, affectionate to arrogant. As might be guessed, Siamese demand a lot of attention and become very jealous if attention is not forthcoming. In return, they are devoted pets that most often become attached to one person in particular, even showing indifference to other people in the house. If separated from this person, it is capable of allowing itself to die.

Owing to their love of liberty and inquisitive nature, Siamese may stray from home, so it is best to restrict their freedom and take them for a walk on a leash with a harness, which they adore, though they are not likely to heel. A large wire run starting from inside the house is the best solution. If they don't get out now and then, Siamese, in frustration, may bare their claws and leap from one piece of furniture to another, perhaps hitting the drapes in between. Generally, though, they are genial animals, exuberant in play, intrusive in all household activities, brave, and trainable. A mature Siamese is unlikely to welcome a young addition, but there are occasional cases of peaceful coexistence.

Siamese queens are the original sexy cats. They reach puberty earlier than do other breeds, commencing calling already at five months, though it's better to wait till they are nine months old to mate them. Their howls and yowls can be annoying, but they generally have larger litters than other breeds, so the noise is worth it.

The precocious kittens develop rapidly, opening their eyes when they are only a few days old and leaving the nesting box at three to four weeks. Born nearly white, they gradually develop their points, the full color appearing only when the cat is nearly an adult. Their eyes change from baby blue to the brilliant blue for which they are renowned at about eight weeks. A show Siamese's career lasts as long as its body color remains pale; if it darkens, its show biz career is over.

As to where this splendid feline came from, the only certainty is that it has an Asiatic origin.

The manuscripts known as *The Cat Book Poems*, dating from 1350, contain pictures of beautiful seal point Siamese and include verses describing them as having black tails, feet, and ears, with white hair and reddish eyes. (At night Siamese eyes shine red, while other cats' eyes are green.) These books are now kept in the Thai National Library in Bangkok, after being saved from Ayudha. which was Siam's capital until it was burned down by invading Burmese in 1767. This proves that the Siamese was a well-loved cat in that ancient city.

There are also legends which explain the origin of the Siamese, its crossed eyes and its kinky tail.

One story says they were bred by the kings of Siam and used as palace guards, pacing on top of the walls and leaping on the backs of intruders.

Another story states the sacred Siamese temple cats were left in charge of a very valuable vase and, to guard it well, they wrapped their tails around it and stared at it so hard that their eyes became crossed.

A third tale explains the origin of the kinked tail. The royal princesses of Siam relied on their cats to look after their rings, and these were kept on the cats' tails; the kinks developed to prevent the rings from falling off.

While these are all possible explanations, scientists have discovered that the squinty and crossed eyes, along with the kinked tail, seem to be linked to the Siamese gene.

GROOMING

One essential of proper care of the cat is grooming. While shorthaired cats can manage most of their own grooming, using their rough tongue, the longhaired cats cannot. Anyone who obtains a longhair breed, such as a Persian or Himalayan, also accepts the responsibility of spending from ten to 30 minutes a day brushing the cat. Special combs and brushes are readily available at any pet shop. The chore can be very pleasant with a cat which is accustomed to the comb. If, however, the cat has not been brushed on a regular basis since it was a kitten, it can be an extremely painful job for both the cat and owner. Should the cat's coat be neglected for too long, it will develop mats, and at that point it would be better for a professional groomer or veterinary office to handle the job. Eventually the coat will grow out again, but the cat does not appreciate the process of combing and the cutting out of severe matting.

Facing page: **Grooming should be a part of every cat's daily regimen — particularly the longhaired variety *below*, or its coat will tangle and mat. The proper grooming tools can be found at your local pet store.** *Right:* **A well-groomed household pet.**

Regular grooming improves your cat's health by controlling fleas and reducing hairballs. Just look at the healthy 15-year old cat *at left*! Meanwhile, this household pet *(above)* happily claws its scratching post.

One positive aspect of proper grooming of a cat is the control of shedding. A cat which has been brushed on a regular basis will shed less hair on the carpet, furniture and owner. Fleas will also be easier to control since the owner will be aware of the presence of a flea infestation earlier, at a much more controllable stage. Yet another benefit of grooming is that it helps to reduce the formation of hairballs in the cat's digestive tract.

The cat normally sheds in cycles which are controlled by the length of days. If the cat is exposed to natural light only, it will shed in the spring and the fall. Should a cat seem to be shedding excessively a veterinarian should be consulted to check the animal for possible medical problems such as fleas, an allergy, ringworm or diet deficiencies.

Another part of grooming which some owners swear *by*, and

others swear *at*, is bathing. While some cats do not mind a bath, others will object violently, and it is not recommended that anyone take the chance of permanent scarring from their pet's claws. The main thing to remember in bathing any cat is to avoid submerging it. It may panic and claw in an attempt to escape. A kitten will adjust fairly easily to the bath. Start when the kitten is about six months old.

The recommended procedure for bathing a cat is as follows: First, using only warm water, fill two basins in the bathtub. Then carefully grasp the cat by the back of the neck, supporting its hindquarters with the other hand. Keep the cat's back toward you with your arm extended. Lift it into one basin. Hopefully the cat will not panic.

Next pour handfuls of water over the cat. Start at the neck, gently soaping the fur from the neck down. This will help prevent any fleas in the coat from running up to the cat's head and ears. Be sure the coat is thoroughly soaked and then rinse, using the water from the second pan. Do not splash the water or the cat may become frightened and try to escape. Rinse all the lather from the fur. Using a wet washcloth, wash the cat's face, ears and head. Two bits of cotton in the ears will keep water out. Also, a drop of mineral oil in each eye will help avoid irritation if the cat struggles and gets soap in its eyes. A constant stream of low-voiced praise may also help keep the cat under control.

A word of warning. Some cats cannot be bathed. DO NOT ATTEMPT TO BATHE THE CAT IF IT IS OBVIOUSLY PANICKED! Even the gentlest animal can inflict severe injury to the eyes, hands and face of its owner! For cats who will not tolerate a bath in water, a veterinarian can recommend dry shampoos to sprinkle into the coat, which are then brushed out after the recommended period of time.

Another important part of grooming concerns the claws. Normally cats have five toes on their forefeet and four on their hind feet. Each toe has a very sharp claw which can be retracted. The claws continue to grow throughout the cat's lifetime and, as time passes, the cat may try to wear the claws down, decorating the furniture with long, unattractive scratches. Cats can be encouraged to use a scratching post instead of the furniture. Often a log cut lengthwise will suffice. Scratching posts can be bought at pet stores but the cat would probably prefer the rough bark. For some cats a scratching post will not be enough to wear the claws down. In these instances a professional clipping may be necessary. A very gentle cat can be clipped by its owner, but be sure not to clip within one-eighth inch of the claw's blood vein. If this is injured the cat will probably never allow the owner to touch its claws again.

One last part of grooming is often neglected by owners. Just like a child, the cat's teeth should be brushed as often as the cat will tolerate. If begun as a kitten, the operation will be simpler. A cat properly cared for will live for many years and its teeth should last its lifetime.

Grooming can be a pleasurable experience for both cat and owner. The cat enjoys the extra attention and the owner has the benefit of the admiration of friends and relatives. A rewarding experience for all concerned!

Left, above and below: **Cat care should also include brushing your cat's teeth occasionally. A solution of water and baking soda will do the job nicely, but begin the practice when your cat is still a kitten. Although most cats object to baths, they don't mind a little water if it involves fishing** *(facing page).*

SINGAPURA

The Singapura is known as a cat having common sense because it seldom squabbles — a quality which has doubtless helped it survive in the streets and drains of Singapore, where it is at home. Due to some people in Singapore not being overly fond of cats, the 'drain cat,' as the Singapura is also called, went relatively unappreciated until some foreigners started adopting the little vagabonds.

Perhaps owing to its deprived background, the Singapura is smaller than other domestic cats, females weighing four pounds or less and males six pounds or less. Like the Abyssinian, it is a ticked* cat, but it is smaller and has different features. It has a medium long, muscular body, with a slightly arched back, a short, rather thick neck, high shoulder blades, and a medium length tail, set upon intermediate long legs and small, tight paws; the head is round, with wide-set, large, expressive, hazel, green or gold, almond-shaped eyes. The Singapura's head is topped off with big, slightly pointed ears, wide open at the base; the muzzle is medium-short with a definite whisker break and there is a full chin.

Singapuras have fine, short, silky fur, with brown ticking on an old ivory ground. The muzzle, chin, chest and stomach are a pale fawn, while the ears, nose and nose bridge are pale to dark salmon; the paw pads are rosy brown.

Singapuras, having street cats as progenitors, are naturally reserved and wary, but once they know no harm is intended they become more responsive and trusting — though they always remain somewhat shy. Singapuras are loving, playful, inquisitive charmers, who involve themselves in all facets of family life. Having lived on the streets for generations, they can adapt to anything, but patient, calm owners in a quiet environment make these cats feel most secure.

There is a waiting list for Singapura kittens, which mature slowly and often do not climb out of the nesting box until they are five weeks old. Certainly, they are not encouraged to leave by their doting mothers, who would willingly nurse them until the next litter is due.

This natural Southeast Asian breed was first brought to the United States in 1975 and shown in 1977. It has been accepted for championship status in all associations except the CFA, where it is registerable.

In Singapore these waifs with the wistful expression come in several more colors, but so far only the ticked variety has been brought to the United States.

*Ticked means having small, contrasting spots of color on the coat of a mammal or the feathers of a bird.

These pages: **The Singapura Cat.**

SNOWSHOE

The Snowshoe got its name from the white mittens on its dark legs. It is also sometimes called a 'Silver Lace' for the same reason. In fact, the Snowshoe looks like a shorthaired Birman, but, unlike the Birman, it also has a white muzzle. *(See Birman)*

When two Siamese cats produced three females with white feet at the Kensing Cattery in Philadelphia in the mid-1960s, a gleam came into the eyes of cat fanciers there and they began a breeding program.

About 10 years later, in the mid-1970s, two breeders in the Midwest and another in Virginia continued developing the breed. American Shorthair bicolors (black and white or blue and white) and Siamese (Seal or Blue point) were crossed. The resulting breed combines the heavier body of the American Shorthair with the slimmer body of the Siamese. Great care is taken in the choice of American shorthair when doing first generation crosses. The cat must exhibit a very strict white pattern conforming to the ideal pattern of the Snowshoe standard. First generation litters are actually Oriental Shorthairs—all solid or bicolor solid—but are registered as Snowshoes. Using only the bicolor kittens and breeding them to a Siamese will produce second generation litters of solids, bicolor solids, pointed and bicolor pointed kittens. From this point, bicolor pointed cats can be bred to other bicolor pointed cats, Siamese, American or Domestic Shorthairs, or Oriental Shorthairs. These litters will contain pointed and bicolor pointed kittens in the first two breeding combinations, and all four patterns in the case of the latter breedings. Eventually, through selective breeding, breeding bicolor pointed cat to bicolor pointed cat should produce only bicolor pointed kittens. However, some pointed kittens still appear occasionally. All generations and all kittens in a litter, from the first generation on, are registered as Snowshoes. Eventually, most breedings will be only Snowshoe to Snowshoe.

Average weight is seven to 13 pounds for females and nine to 18 pounds for males. Head type is a modified wedge (nearly an equilateral triangle), with a dip or stop at the nose bridge forming a two-planed head. The eyes are brilliant blue, large, oval and slanted toward the ears. The ears are large and pointed. The body type is medium-boned, large and long, and hefty compared to the Oriental body type. The only acceptable show colors are Seal and Blue. White

patterning is a full white muzzle, forming an inverted 'V' on the nose and ending at the nose bridge. A white chin, chest and stomach should be part of the pattern. Front legs should be solid white up to the ankle; hind legs should be solid white up to the hock. The coat is short and glossy, with colorpoints at the mask, ears, legs, tail, and white feet. Several pattern variations are allowed and are discussed in the standard.

The Snowshoe was advanced to championship status by the CFA on 1 May 1983. Since then, three Snowshoes have obtained their championships. There are currently twelve active breeders in various parts of the country who are working for general recognition of the Snowshoe breed throughout the cat fancy.

Snowshoes are loving, people-oriented cats who follow their owners everywhere, for they dislike being left alone. They are soft-spoken and make excellent house pets.

This fairly new breed is a rarity even in North America and currently nonexistent elsewhere.

SOMALI

Somalis are longhaired Abyssinians, and the standard is the same as for the Abyssinian, except that they have medium long and silky, ticked fur, exaggerated ear tufts, and a fox-like tail.

When longhaired kittens first started appearing in Abyssinian litters in the 1960s, some breeders claimed that out-crosses to longhaired breeds must have occurred. Later it was discovered, however, that certain breeding lines of Abyssinians have carried the recessive, longhair gene for many generations. Through inbreeding, the recessive gene became dominant and voilà!—longhaired Abys. This longhair gene must be present in both parents to produce Somalis.

A Somali crossed with an Abyssinian will have shorthaired kittens carrying the gene for long hair. Mated together, these plusher-coated, shorthaired cats will create some shorthaired and some longhaired
continued on page 177

Below left: **The ticking on these Somali kittens will become more pronounced as they grow older. Note the characteristic large and expressive eyes on the kitten** *below. Facing page:* **An adult Somali.**

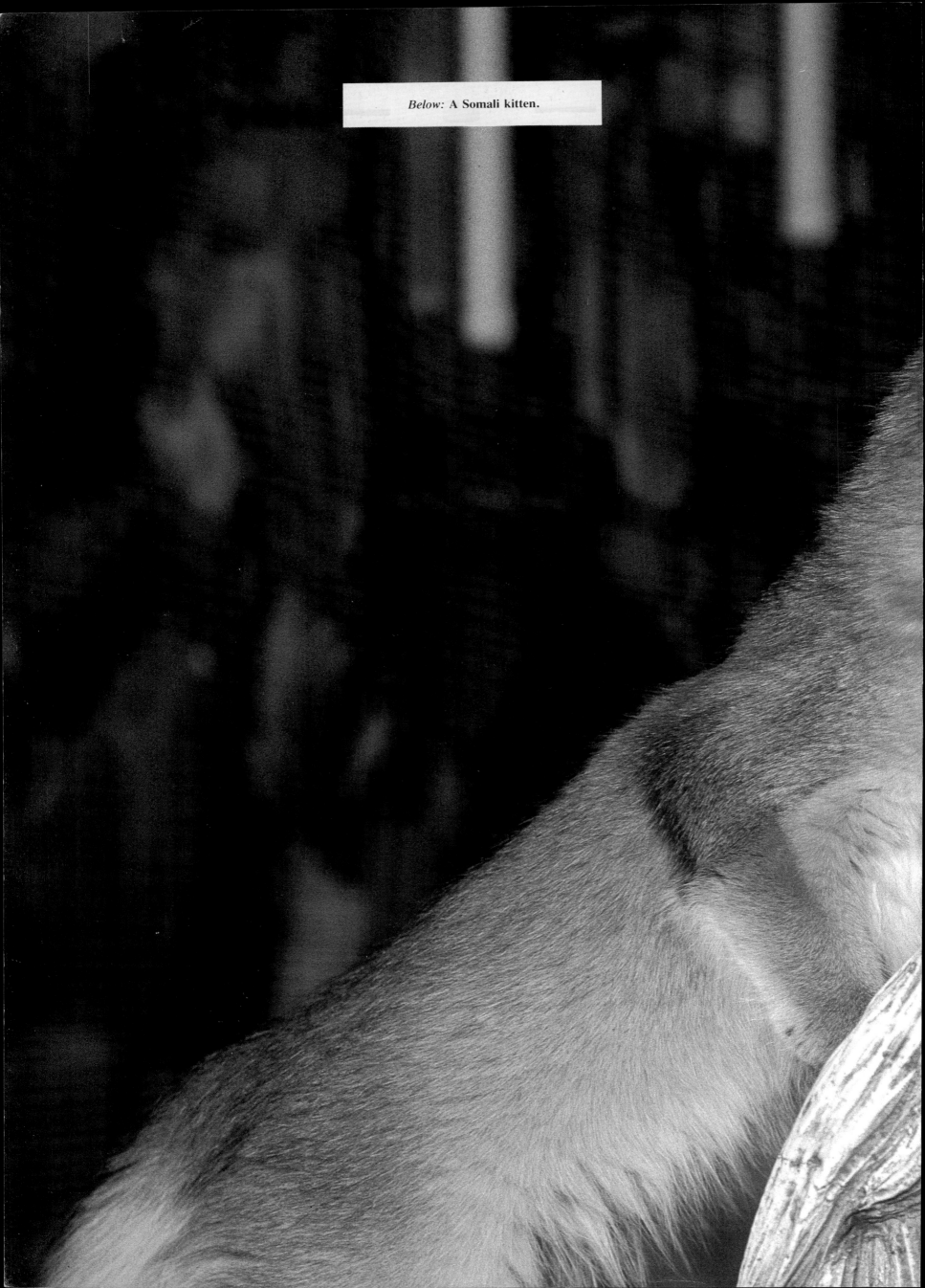

Below: A Somali kitten.

These pages: **The Somali, looking much like its regal cousin, the lion.**

continued from page 172
offspring, all of whom must be registered as Somalis in North America, even though they are genetically identical to many Abyssinians, which may also carry the longhair gene.

Some Abyssinian breeders neutered the longhaired kittens born in their litters to keep the Abyssinian breed pure, while others, finding the long hair attractive, decided to develop the new breed; Somalis achieved CFA championship status in 1978.

The previous year, a German cat fancier had imported some Somalis and the breed was officially presented to Europe. Prior to that time, longhaired Abyssinians had been bred in both Europe and Australia. A Somali, as a matter of fact, was exhibited as early as 1965 in Australia.

Outwardly, Somalis resemble Abyssinians in looking like a wild cat, and they are both athletic cats, needing some space in which to exercise their well-muscled bodies (a terrace or a garden will do nicely), but they are also intelligent, gentle, and soft-spoken, and enjoy the company of humans and other pets.

Somali queens have small litters: three or four tiny, dark kittens which do not attain their full beauty until they are about 18 months old. While only two colors — ruddy and red — are currently accepted, breeders are producing other colors — blue, silver, lilac — which may be recognized in the future, especially since there is evidence that the earliest Abyssinians came in more than two colors.

SPHYNX

Although this cat is extremely loving and sweet-natured, and purrs constantly, it's not for everyone. The Sphynx needs a special owner who will give it lots of body contact, which it adores, and keep it out of draughts, or it will catch serious colds. In fact, because this cat is utterly hairless, except for thin down in the wintertime, it should usually wear a sweater. This *chat sans poils* (cat without hair) requires frequent feedings owing to its high (four degrees higher than most other breeds') body temperature, but the Sphynx can eat all it wants without gaining any weight because it doesn't store any fat.

The origin of the hairless cat is somewhat mysterious. Some say the first one was born in South America. It is thought that the Aztec Indians had hairless cats, and the Mexican hairless, now extinct, was bred in Mexico in the late 1800s. Hairless kittens resembling the Sphynx have appeared in litters of various breeds in France, England and Canada. However, it was an alert owner in Ontario, Canada in 1966 who started the Sphynx breed after a hairless kitten was born in a normal litter there.

These 'Canadian Hairless,' as they are also called, are quite rare, since Sphynx-to-Sphynx matings have not produced hairless kittens, and most known examples of the breed have been found as strays or adopted 'accidents.' According to one expert, a Sphynx crossed with a domestic shorthair will result in wiry-haired, curly-haired, and hairless kittens, though there is little likelihood of the latter. Partially-hairless cats have appeared in some Rex breeding programs, but were regarded as non-viable Rex cats and Sphynx cats.

Occasionally a Sphynx is seen at a cat show, where the standard is for tough, wrinkled, hairless skin, a sweet facial expression, expressive eyes (usually gold), huge ears, a long, camel-backed torso, long legs, and a long, whip-like tail. All colors and patterns are acceptable and these look like tattoos, since the cat has no hair. The sum of these characteristics is for many the opposite of almost all they admire in the cat.

Although the Sphynx is recognized today as a pedigreed breed by a few of the smaller North American cat associations, it has not been accepted by the CFA.

Pages 178 – 181: **The mysterious and unusual Sphynx.**

TIFFANY

The Tiffany is a longhaired Burmese which comes in sable only with gold eyes. The coat is medium long and silky, similar to that of the Turkish Angora *(See Turkish Angora)*. It has a modified neck ruff and a fox-like facial expression, with rounded eyes.

The first Tiffanies were produced in England during early attempts to develop solid chocolate Himalayans (now called Kashmirs), when Himalayans and Burmese were crossed. Once thought to be a spontaneous mutation, the Tiffany is now known to be the result of a recessive longhair gene.

Because during the past 20 years fewer and fewer longhaired, sable kittens have been born in Burmese litters, the Tiffany has become a rarified breed.

A Florida cat fancier, who introduced the Tiffany to the United States, is still the only person perpetuating the breed here. For lack of numbers, it is not currently registered in any association.

Tiffanies chirp, rather than meow, and enjoy conversations with their owners. They are gentle and playful, similar to Burmese, but less active and more docile. *(See Burmese)*

TONKINESE

A hybrid cross between a Siamese and a Burmese, the Tonkinese combines the best of both breeds. The dark points blend gently into the body color, which is intermediate between Siamese and Burmese coloring. It is moderate in every physical aspect, has exquisite aqua eyes, and is friendly and full of fun.

The first known Tonkinese, although she isn't officially recognized as such, is thought to be *Wong Mau*, ancestress of the Burmese. There are, however, documents which indicate that the chocolate Siamese exhibited in England in the late 1800s were also Siamese-Burmese hybrids.

From the 1950s through the early 1970s, various American and Canadian breeders developed the breed. The Tonkinese was first registered by the Canadian Cat Association in 1974. It was accepted by the Cat Fanciers Association in 1978 and received championship status in 1984. Several other associations in North America, Europe, and Australia have since recognized it.

'Tonks,' as they are also known, come in five gorgeous colors: natural mink, a warm brown coat with seal points; honey mink, a

Below and facing page: **Crossing the Burmese and the Siamese produced a new breed — the luxuriously coated Tonkinese.**

These pages: **The Tonkinese Cat.**

ruddy brown coat with seal points; champagne mink, a beige coat with light brown points; blue mink, a blue-grey coat with slate-blue points; and platinum mink, a silver coat with darker silver points. Their fur, which is short, soft, shiny, and close-lying, feels like mink.

These beautiful cats have medium-sized bodies with long legs, the hind legs a little longer than the front ones, and long, tapering tails. Their heads are moderately triangular in shape and are accented by alert looking, rounded ears and open, almond-shaped, blue-green eyes. There is a slight dip between the eyes and a pinch at the whiskers.

Tonks are known as cats with personality. They tend to be mischievous and should not be trusted around bird cages. Aerial artists, they especially like climbing and jumping so, when kept indoors, cat trees are in order. A Tonkinese alone in a wire run with a roof and shelves at varying heights will amuse itself for hours, racing up and down and leaping from one shelf to another. These are loving, loyal, outgoing, curious, and vocal felines which get along well with children, other cats and dogs.

Today, Tonkinese are bred only to other Tonkinese, producing 50 percent Tonkinese, 25 percent Siamese, and 25 percent Burmese. The non-Tonkinese progeny make wonderful pets.

TURKISH ANGORA

Angoras are treated with great respect in Turkey because there is a legend that Ataturk, the renowned general and president who brought Turkey into the modern world, will one day return as an odd-eyed, deaf Turkish Angora. These graceful street cats were named after the old city of Angora, now Ankara.

They were the first longhaired cats to appear in Europe, arriving in Italy and France in the sixteenth century, when they were greatly admired. For a time, they were known as French cats. Later on, this breed also appeared in England.

In the nineteenth century, when the first cat shows began, creating a general interest in cats, an attempt was made to differentiate Angoras from other longhaired cats. An English writer of 1868 pictured the Angora as 'a beautiful variety with silvery hair of fine texture, generally longest on the neck, but also on the tail.' But people preferred the more recently arrived Persians, and soon the Turkish type was in eclipse.

By the turn of the century, only a few Angoras remained in Turkey, as the breeding stock had largely been diluted through crossings with Persians, perhaps to improve the Persian coat. In Turkey they were still appreciated, but they disappeared in other parts of the world until after World War II, when there was a revival of interest in these elegant felines and new breeding programs were started in America, Britain and Sweden.

The CFA recognized Angoras for full championship competition in the early 1970s; at first only white Angoras were accepted, but since 1978 Angoras in a wide range of colors may compete. Not wanting to rely on obtaining cats from Turkey, since there were so few left, the British elected to create their own Angora cats through a scientific breeding program based on genetic principles. They have succeeded marvelously except that their Angoras speak with a Siamese voice.

Angoras differ from Persians in both confirmation and fur. Angoras are long, graceful, and lithe, with medium length, silky hair, and have no thick undercoat. Persians, on the other hand, are cobby, solid, and round, with long, thick hair and a woolly undercoat. The Angora is medium sized, with fine, yet strong, bones, long legs, and

Right: **The Turkish Angora Cat.**

Above: **A beautiful white Turkish Angora.** *Right:* **The Turkish Angora has a lithe, graceful body with a long and full tail.**

dainty, tufted toes. Its head is wedge shaped, with large, erect, tufted ears, almond-shaped eyes and a gently rounded chin. It has a long, well-plumed and tapering tail. Sometimes, when the cat is in motion, the tail is carried horizontally over the body almost touching the head.

As with other blue-eyed, white cats, some of the white Angoras are born deaf, so it is wise to have a kitten checked before buying it. If you do get a deaf cat, it's best not to let it go outside unsupervised because there is more risk of its getting hit by a car since it can't hear the car coming. Although white is still the favorite color, Turkish Angoras today are accepted in black, blue, black smoke, blue smoke, silver tabby, red tabby, brown tabby, calico, and bicolor as well.

Angoras are well-behaved, sweet house cats. Because they like to remain still for long periods of time, they have a sphinx-like quality. Intelligent, they can be easily trained to retrieve and perform tricks. Angoras love water and like to play in the bathtub.

Turkish Van cats, a true-breeding variety within the breed which developed in the area of Lake Van in Turkey, enjoy water even more and are seen there swimming in shallow streams. These native cats, which are still rare and expensive, are white with striking auburn faces and tails.

Below: A gallery of cats—A Maine Coon, an Abyssinian, a Siamese and a Persian. *Overleaf:* A look all cat owners have seen before—Something has caught this cat's attention. Is it a bird, a plane, a leaf or something we mere mortals simply cannot see?